WOODWORKER'S
Pattern Book
Updated & Expanded 2nd Edition

Over 100 Realistic Animal Designs

Jacob and Wayne Fowler

FOX CHAPEL
PUBLISHING

A Scroll Saw Woodworking & Crafts Book
www.scrollsawer.com

Dedication

For Heather, my wife and Jacob's mother. Your continual support, understanding, and honest criticism have always led to better designs and finished work.

© 2025 by Wayne Fowler, Jacob Fowler, and Fox Chapel Publishing Company, Inc.

Woodworker's Pattern Book, Updated & Expanded 2nd Edition is a revised edition of *Woodworker's Pattern Book*, first published in 2016 by Fox Chapel Publishing Company, Inc. The patterns contained herein are copyrighted by the author. Readers may make copies of these patterns for personal use. The patterns themselves, however, are not to be duplicated for resale or distribution under any circumstances. Any such copying is a violation of copyright law.

ISBN 978-1-4971-0486-0

The Cataloging-in-Publication Data is on file with the Library of Congress.

Managing Editor: Gretchen Bacon
Acquisitions Editor: Kaylee J. Schofield
Editor: Joseph Borden
Designer: Wendy Reynolds
Proofreader: Kelly Umenhofer

To learn more about the other great books from Fox Chapel Publishing, or to find a retailer near you, call toll-free 800-457-9112, send mail to 903 Square Street, Mount Joy, PA 17552, or visit us at *www.FoxChapelPublishing.com*.

We are always looking for talented authors. To submit an idea, please send a brief inquiry to acquisitions@foxchapelpublishing.com.

Printed in China
First printing

Introduction

Jacob drew his first fretwork pattern as a teenager. The detailed owl was based on a photo he pulled from the Internet and interpreted using drawing software on his computer. There were a few structural issues with the design, but they were easily fixed, and I cut the piece. Our wildlife exploration had begun.

We live near Toronto, Canada, with its many zoos and wildlife preserves. Digital cameras in hand, away we went. Over the years, we have visited the Toronto Zoo, several private zoos, and a very large wildlife preserve with hundreds of lions, elephants, zebras, hippos, rhinos, and dozens of other types of animals and birds. We found a falconry centre that raises and displays many birds of prey with little or no cages. We went to Las Vegas to see the tigers at the Mirage; took many trips to Florida for alligators, osprey, and dozens of types of shore birds; and visited the family cottage for the smaller critters, like bullfrogs or chipmunks. We took thousands of pictures that Jacob worked into hundreds of patterns, which improved as the pictures got better. The latest example from Florida, an osprey taking flight, is included in this book.

Jacob does not trace the wildlife. Instead, he interprets the animals, often using features from multiple photos to avoid shadows and to take advantage of different angles and lighting. This also helps him achieve our goal of ensuring that each design is a freestanding single piece of wood after it is cut; using multiple angles helps him avoid placing cuts close to the edges.

We also strive to make the finished designs as realistic as possible, so some of the patterns are very complex. (You might find yourself muttering a few discouraging words about Jacob while cutting these projects.) But when all is said and done, the finished piece usually looks so good that working through Jacob's complex pattern is worth it.

We hope that you will find these designs both challenging and rewarding. Good cutting!

—**Wayne Fowler**

We travel all over Canada and the United States to photograph birds and animals. Jacob chooses the best features from an assortment of photos when he creates each pattern. I select wood that complements the design and cut the artwork.

About the Authors

Wayne Fowler, a retired information technology manager, began scrolling 27 years ago after seeing scroll saws for the first time at a Toronto woodworking show with his father-in-law, Tom Poppleton. When his mother-in-law, Pat, asked him to buy a saw for Tom's birthday, Wayne bought one for himself, too. He started by adapting designs to create painted pine puzzles and was selling everything he could make by Christmas of his first year of cutting. Over the next few years, he tried all sorts of scrolling before shifting to fretwork and natural wood, thanks to the acquisition of a high-end saw that made detailed fretwork easier. Wayne published his first article, about his puzzles, in 1998. Over the next 18 years, he published almost 150 magazine articles, most in partnership with his son and pattern designer, Jacob, about everything from detailed fret patterns to cutting metal with a scroll saw. Wayne's work has won awards at his local craft guild, a scroll saw picnic, and several science-fiction convention art shows.

Jacob Fowler made his first design for a scroll saw at age 5. It was a whale bank, because his father collected whale art. About 10 years later, Jacob restarted his design career by cleaning up many of Wayne's puzzle patterns and drawing mainly fantasy puzzle patterns meant to challenge his father's ability to follow twisting lines. One night, he decided to try doing fret designs on his computer; he took a public domain picture of an owl and made it into a fret design using drawing software. After a series of iterative pattern developments, he and his father started taking pictures of wildlife in the wild, at local zoos, and even in Las Vegas, and turning them into fret patterns. Jacob also continued to draw many original designs by hand, mainly with fantasy themes, and converting them on his PC. Along the way, he published more than 200 of his 1,000 designs in partnership with his father in magazine articles as well as pattern packs and special projects.

Both Wayne and Jacob take wildlife photos mainly, but not exclusively, in zoos and other wildlife preserves. Jacob does all of the design work, and Wayne proofs the patterns to ensure they can be cut. Wayne cuts and finishes the projects and writes any articles or text associated with any publications.

Contents

BIG CATS

PREDATORS

BIRDS OF PREY

BACKYARD ANIMALS

EXOTIC ANIMALS

Gallery

Alert Tiger
(Page 25)

Dire Wolf

(Page 55)

Wolf Stare

(Page 48)

Bass-Voice Bullfrog

(Page 102)

Savanna Stripes — Zebra

(Page 118)

Running Horse
(Page 100)

White Rhino
(Page 125)

Golden Eagle
(Page 70)

Bald Eagle Portrait

(Page 67)

Screech Owl

(Page 75)

Majestic Buck
(Page 97)

Grey Squirrel
(Page 87)

Coyote Oval
(Page 60)

American Robin
(Page 85)

**Jackrabbit
with Base**
(Page 105)

Delicate Fawn
(Page 96)

Forest-Dwelling Moose
(Page 99)

Raccoon
(Page 86)

River Hippo Walking
(Page 121)

Shy Gorilla
(Page 112)

Wary Rhinoceros
(Page 116)

Giraffe Bust

(Page 110)

Tips & Techniques

Here are a few hints and tips based on my experience that should make cutting, finishing, and presenting the designs in this book more successful. If you are already cutting at this level, just skip this section and start cutting! There is no "right" way to do this, ultimately, just your way.

Wood

In most cases, you can use ¼" to ¾" (6mm to 19mm)-thick wood to cut these designs. However, there are a few other factors to consider in choosing wood, including its grain pattern and direction, and how hard it is.

Selecting the Wood

Because the patterns are very detailed, you will need to use wood that will "hold" the pattern features. I suggest using hardwoods, such as cherry, oak, sycamore, or ash, because softer varieties will break or chip as you cut the patterns. I happen to live where there are lots of hardwood trees, and I know several folks who harvest unusual hardwoods that don't have much grain. When I was making the samples for this book, I was able to use Eastern cottonwood, box elder, walnut, beech, and elm, in addition to the basic varieties of hardwood. Check with your favorite suppliers, either local or those who advertise in *Scroll Saw Woodworking & Crafts* magazine, to find appropriate wood.

Use hardwoods for these patterns because they will "hold" the features. Softer varieties of wood will break or chip as you cut the intricate designs.

A second factor to consider is how bold the grain is and whether it complements or distracts from the design. For most of the patterns in the gallery, I tried to use wood with lighter features in the primary piece, while choosing bolder grain for the bases or backing boards so the design was highlighted.

Choose a grain that complements the design. I like to use wood with lighter features for the fretwork and a piece with bolder grain for the backing board.

Next, consider how hard the wood actually is. For harder woods, such as ash, consider using thinner wood, which will cause less burning and cut more quickly than thicker wood.

Finally, examine the direction of the grain. Although we have not marked the patterns for placement on the wood, you should usually place rectangular designs with their long sides lengthwise with the grain and patterns, such as birds of prey, on their sides along the grain.

Place rectangular patterns with their long side parallel to the grain. Place odd-shaped patterns, like birds, on their sides with the grain.

Preparing the Wood

After you roughly cut a piece of wood for the pattern, cover it with clear packing tape. This often-published hint is extremely valuable. The tape serves three purposes: it makes the pattern easier to remove after cutting, it makes the cutting easier and cleaner, and it extends the life of the blade. I have been told that the latter are results of the plastic in the tape melting and lubricating the blade. I prefer using clear packing tape rather than blue painter's tape because you can see the wood through the tape when you are placing the pattern. To place the tape, I use a bladed dispenser from an office-supply store together with multipacks of tape (I use a lot of tape). Overlap the rows of tape a bit, so the pattern will pull off more easily. Then, attach the pattern with spray adhesive, glue stick, hot glue, etc.

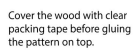

Cover the wood with clear packing tape before gluing the pattern on top.

Tools

In addition to your saw, you'll need blades, a drill and bits, and finishing equipment. I'll cover finishing in a separate section.

Selecting Saw Blades

If you have been cutting detailed fret patterns for some time, I am sure that you have preferences for blades. If you need some advice, here are a few of my suggestions.

There is always a balance between the thickness of the blade, the thickness and hardness of the wood, and the details in the pattern. There is no one "right" blade for these patterns. However, for any of them, you should use nothing bigger than a #5 blade. For most patterns, I use a #2 or #3 blade for the coarser designs and a #2/0, #0, or #1 blade for the details. The simplest way to decide which blade to use is to look at the pattern and choose the smallest blade that you are comfortable using to cut the details. If you are uncomfortable cutting the design with the blade of your choice, try enlarging the pattern until it looks like something you can do.

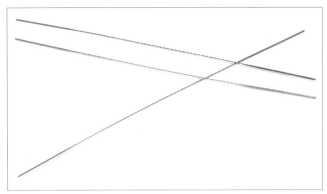

For most patterns, I use a #2 blade for the coarser designs and a #2/0, #0, or #1 blade for the details.

Drill Bits

Bits are not mentioned very often, but are an important factor in successfully cutting the fine features in many patterns.

You need to choose a bit size that you can drill the entry hole in the waste area without harming the wood you want to keep. In general, you are looking for a drill bit that is just slightly larger than the widest dimension of the blade. However, the widths of blades of a particular size/number vary by manufacturer (i.e., a #5 blade from Pégas isn't necessarily the same width as a #5 blade from Olson). Look at the widest blade dimension for a specific brand, match it to the drill bit diameter, and then add a fudge factor so you can easily insert the blade through the hole.

I buy drill bits that are sized in fractions of inches. I generally use a ³⁄₆₄" (1.2mm) bit for #2 to #7 blades and a ¹⁄₃₂" (1mm) bit for #1 and smaller blades. Other folks use numbered drill bits and refer to charts to match the numbers to hole sizes. For example, a #56 bit is

similar to a ³⁄₆₄" (1.2mm) bit, and a #67 bit is roughly equivalent to a ¹⁄₃₂" (1mm) bit. You can drill most of Jacob's designs with these two bits. You may have to use a #69 bit to cut with a #2/0 blade. You can check the bit and blade specifications to match them to each other or simply pick two sizes (e.g., my ¹⁄₃₂" and ³⁄₆₄" (1 and 1.2mm) combination or a #67 and #56 combination).

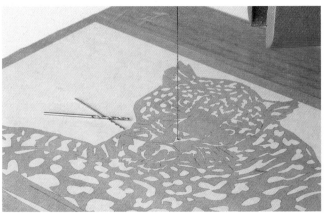

When drilling blade-entry holes, it's important to match the drill bit to the blade. I generally use a ³⁄₆₄" (1.2mm) (or #56) bit for #2 to #7 blades and a ¹⁄₃₂" (1mm) (or #67) bit for #1 and smaller blades.

Cutting the Patterns

In the simplest terms, always cut the middle first, and then work your way to the outside. This strategy works both for the whole pattern (cut the perimeter last) and for portions of designs, such as the face of an animal (start with the eyes and work out to the ears or mouth). The idea is to maintain the integrity of the overall piece while you remove strategic pieces and thereby weaken the structure of the wood.

Three factors will affect your ability to successfully follow the lines in the design. They are:

- The wood. On wood with heavy grain, like oak, there is a natural tendency for the blade to follow the grain and not the lines in the pattern. Be prepared to force the saw where you want it to go rather than let it drift down the grain.
- The speed of the saw. Contrary to intuition, the faster the saw is stroking, the easier it is to control where it is going, because you are pushing the piece rather than letting the saw pull it. You will have more control over a saw running at its top speed than one running at a lower speed, once you understand that you are in control. I only slow my saw to cut very fine details with very fine blades.
- The size of the blade. There is a trade-off here; you have more control over thicker blades, but you can cut finer details with thinner blades. The bottom line is that you should use the largest blade that will let you cut the features in the pattern.

When you start cutting, cut a few simple shapes in the interior of the pattern to get a feel for the combination of wood and blade before you tackle more complicated areas, such as the eyes.

Years ago, I had an issue with my interior cuts warping—the back of the fret was different than the front and the waste piece was warped. A wise man, who happened to sell scroll saws, told me that I was pushing too hard; I needed to slow down and just guide the piece along the line. He also told me to change my blades more often, because dull blades can cause warping. You can buy blades for about 25 cents each, so throwing away dull blades is a low-cost way to better cuts. So, if you feel like you are pushing too hard, relax and change the blade.

Finally, keep this piece of advice in mind as you are cutting; I call this the "every one of God's creatures is unique" rule. Sometimes you might not quite follow the lines in a pattern. As long as the slip does not affect the structure of the piece and is not part of a critical feature, such as an eye, no one is going to notice once you take the pattern off.

Finishing the Projects

Your first step in finishing a project is what I call the "dreaded sanding stage." No matter what, sandpaper in some form will have to touch your cut piece; you need strategies for sanding without breaking the bridges.

I usually start by sanding the front and back of the piece with a power sander to remove residual glue from the tape (on the front) and any blade burrs (on the back). I also smooth the perimeters of rectangular and oval pieces. I then run over the interior and exterior edges on both the top and bottom by hand with a folded quarter-sheet of very fine sandpaper (220 or 320 grit). Finally, I clean the piece, using a small paintbrush, reserved for that purpose, to remove the interior sawdust; a used dull blade to push out any interior debris from the cutting; and a clean rag to remove the surface dust.

I am always trying new finishing products, but I tend to gravitate to thin, low-odor oils, such as tung oil. Thin oil is perfect for flowing into the sides of the many frets you have just cut. To protect the piece, oil should cover all surfaces, including the interiors of the frets.

I have also started polishing my finished pieces using carnauba wax and a soft buffing wheel from the Beall Tool Company that attaches to my drill press. The kit that I bought called for a grinder or lathe to spin the wheel, but I found that to be too fast and my drill press is much easier to control with fretwork. And as a bonus, I end up with polished knuckles! You have to be very careful how you hold the piece while polishing it with one hand, always holding the piece firmly on the far side away from the wheel, with the other hand guiding the piece against the wheel. It will take a bit of practice. Start with a few small pieces, but be aware that you may lose a piece until you get the hang of it. One you've got it, though, the finished result looks and feels better, which is important if you are selling your work. One downside is that the buffing wheel will leave a lot of lint on the piece that will either have to be brushed or blown away.

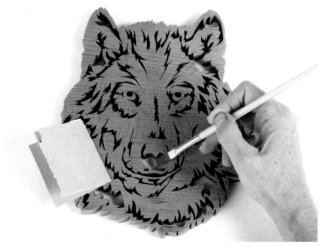

I sand every piece with a power sander, smooth it with sandpaper, and remove sawdust with a paintbrush before adding tung oil finish.

Displaying Your Work

Over the years, I have developed a half-dozen methods for displaying my finished fretwork pieces. Here are some of the most successful suggestions.

Rectangular and Square Designs

To form a stand for projects with straight edges, I often cut two half circles of ¾" (19mm)-thick wood, and then cut a slot the same width as the project in the curved side of each. If the slots are sized correctly, the project should rest safely in the stand without glue. This gives folks who purchase my fretwork the option of displaying it on a shelf or hanging it on a wall.

Another alternative is to make a base of ¾" (19mm)-thick wood. Cut a rectangle that is 2" to 3" (51mm to 76mm) wide and the length of the finished piece plus 1" to 2" (25mm to 51mm). Sand or rout the top edges to soften the corners, and attach the base to the bottom of the project with dowels or screws.

Recently, I have been gluing a backing board to the finished piece. I try to use thinner wood that complements the project. I trace the project and cut the backing board, glue the backing board to the fret piece, and then finish the combined piece (including smoothing out the outside of the combined piece with a sander). I install a self-leveling picture hanger on the back, so the artwork can be hung on a wall.

Given how difficult it is to find thin wide wood these days, I often use thin plywood with some interesting veneer glued to the front for backing boards. I have found veneers readily available at speciality woodshops at a significantly lower price than thin wood. Typically, the same stores sell thin Baltic birch plywood in smaller sheets. I rough cut a piece of plywood for the backing board, and use scissors to rough cut a piece of veneer to the same size. I then use wood glue to glue the veneer and plywood together, using a heavy object (in my case, my box of clamps) on top of the combination until the glue dries. I then glue the backing board to the piece.

Oval and Round Designs

Backing boards (see bottom left) work very well for oval or round designs, and pieces finished in this manner have sold very well for me.

You can also add a base to a round fret piece. Cut an oval that is about 2" (51mm) across and approximately half the length of the artwork when it is positioned upright. Cut a centered slot in the base that is the same width as the fret piece and about half the length of the base. If the artwork fits the slot well, it should rest in the base without glue.

A third way to display a rounded fret piece is to mount it on a pair of pillars that are fixed to a small rectangular or oval base. For the mounting posts, I buy a brass rod (⅛" or ³⁄₁₆" [3 or 5mm]) at the home improvement store and use dull blades to cut it to 1" (25mm) or 1½" (38mm) lengths. Drill two equally spaced holes in the bottom of the finished fret piece, and drill matching holes in the base. This type of display makes a dramatic entry into an art show. The technique also works well for designs cut into "live edge" boards (those with bark attached to the edges). You may need to cut the posts to different lengths and/or adjust the depths of the holes, so the artwork sits level relative to the base.

Naturally Shaped Designs

A number of these designs are shaped to match the animal's profile. Within this group, there are two types of designs: those with a flat bottom and those without.

For the flat-bottomed designs, like the jackrabbit, I cut a simple oval base the same length as the finished fretwork piece. I use a router to give the base a more finished look, but that is a matter of individual taste. Attach the artwork to the base using dowels and glue or wood screws.

For the pieces with uneven bottoms, such as the wolf's head (page 48), I cut simple oval or rectangular backing boards sized to fit the exterior of the artwork. Before you finish the artwork with oil, cut and sand the backing board and glue the fret piece to it. Let the glue dry, and then finish the project with the oil of your choice.

For pieces with straight edges, I like to cut stands or a base. Adding a backing board gives buyers the option to hang the artwork on the wall.

Some naturally shaped designs sit nicely on a base. Others work well glued to a backing board or hung on the wall.

For rounded artwork, cut a base and either rout a slot that fits the fretwork or attach the artwork with screws or posts.

Patterns

Alert Tiger

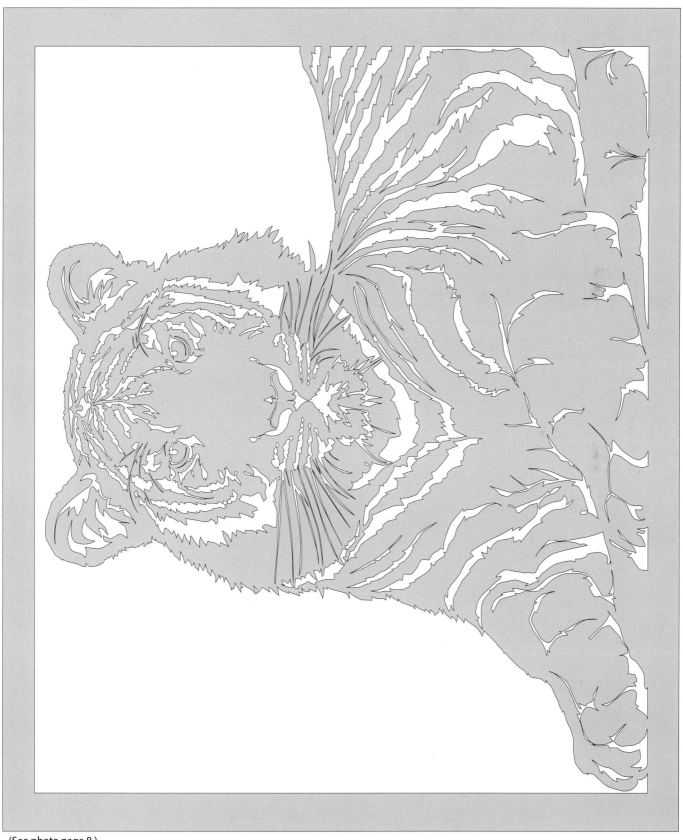

(See photo page 8.)

Sumatran Tiger in Repose

Note: We recommend enlarging this complex pattern by at least 150% to make it easier to cut.

Siberian Tiger on Guard

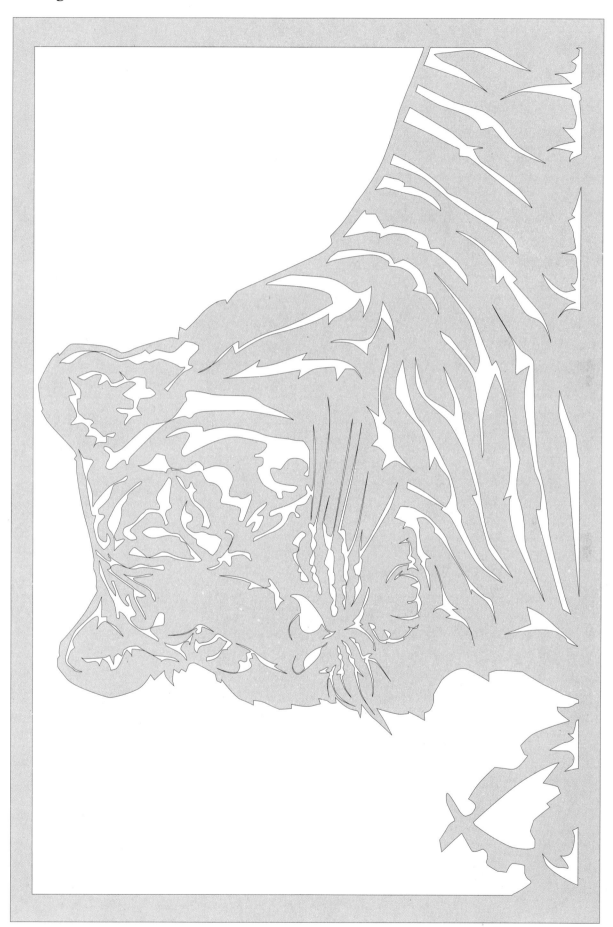

Siberian Tiger Portait

Dignified White Tiger

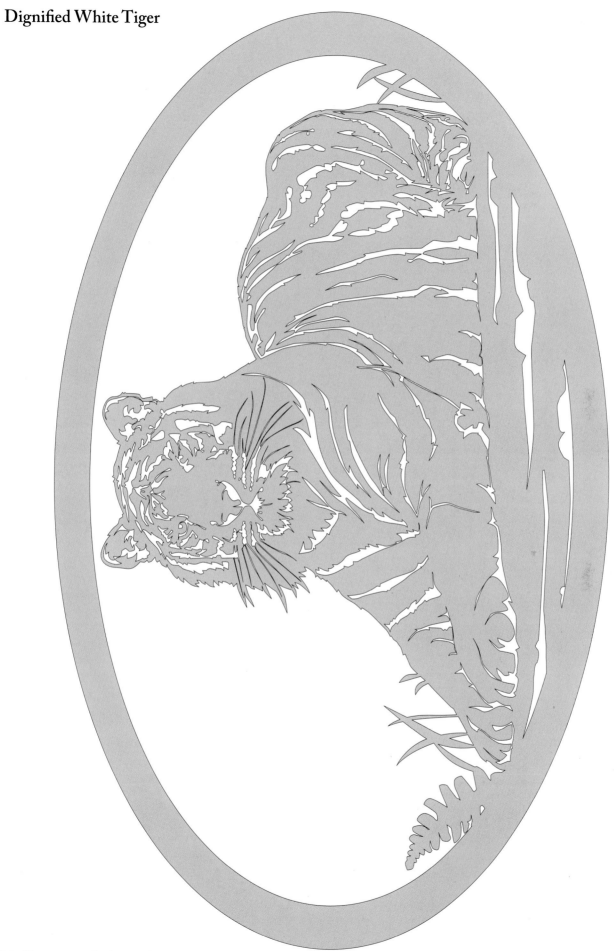

Note: We recommend enlarging this complex pattern by at least 150% to make it easier to cut.

Vigilant Tiger

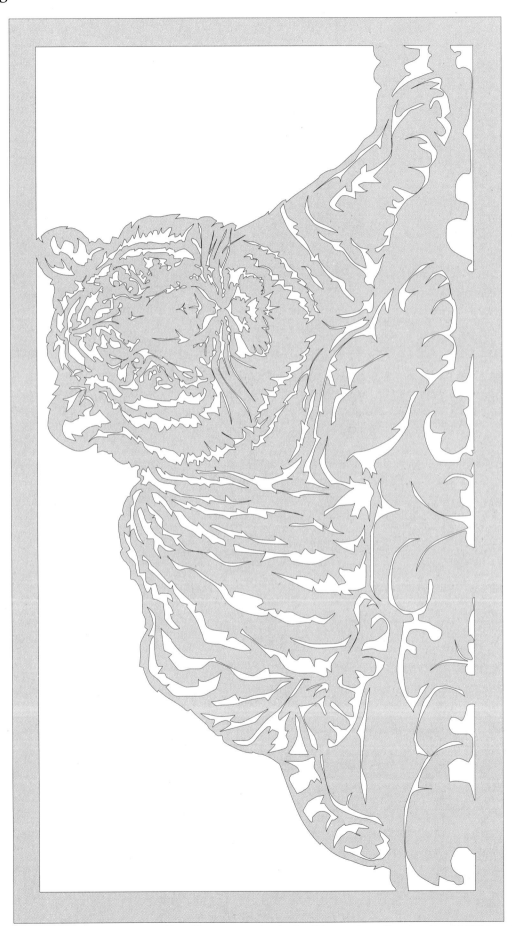

Note: We recommend enlarging this complex pattern by at least 150% to make it easier to cut.

King of the Jungle — Male Lion

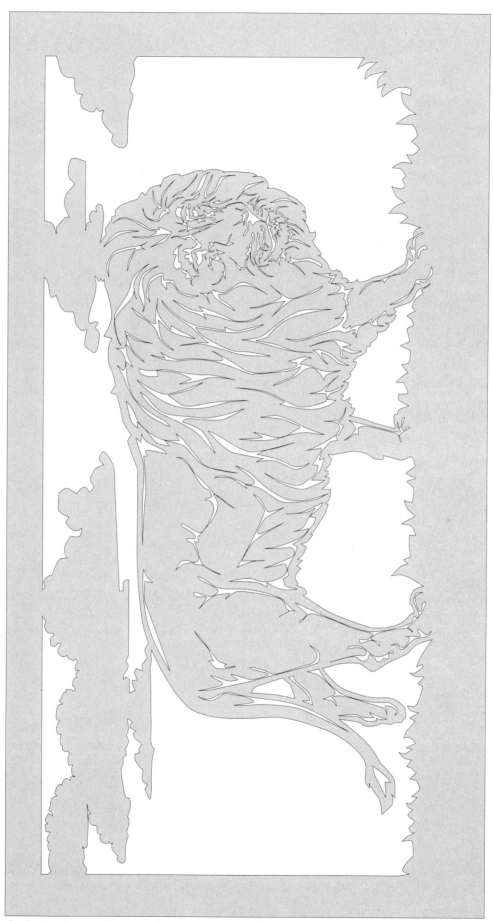

Note: We recommend enlarging this complex pattern by at least 150% to make it easier to cut.

Lion Portrait

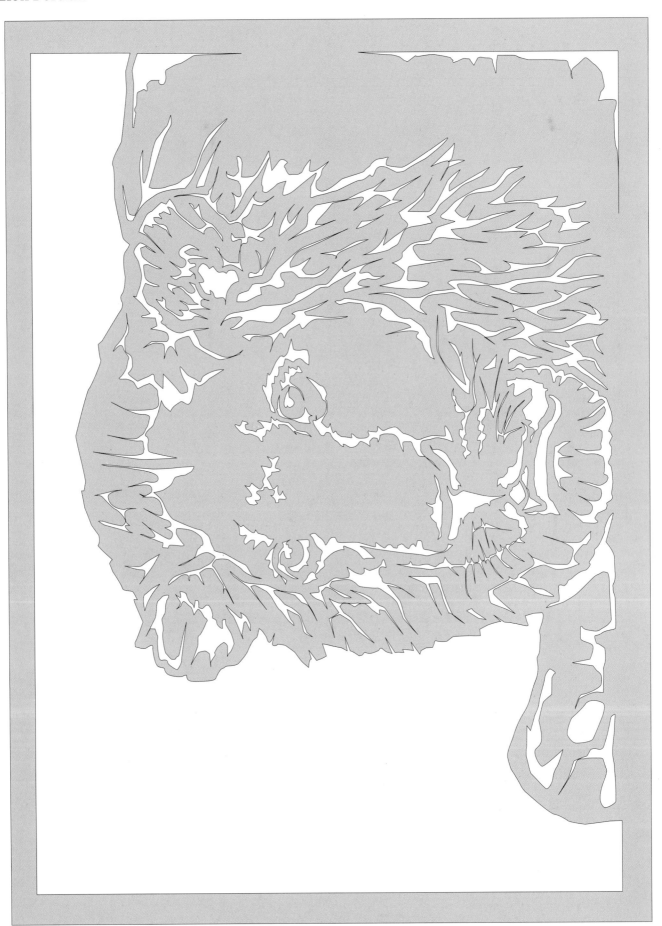

Note: We recommend enlarging this complex pattern by at least 150% to make it easier to cut.

Courting Lions

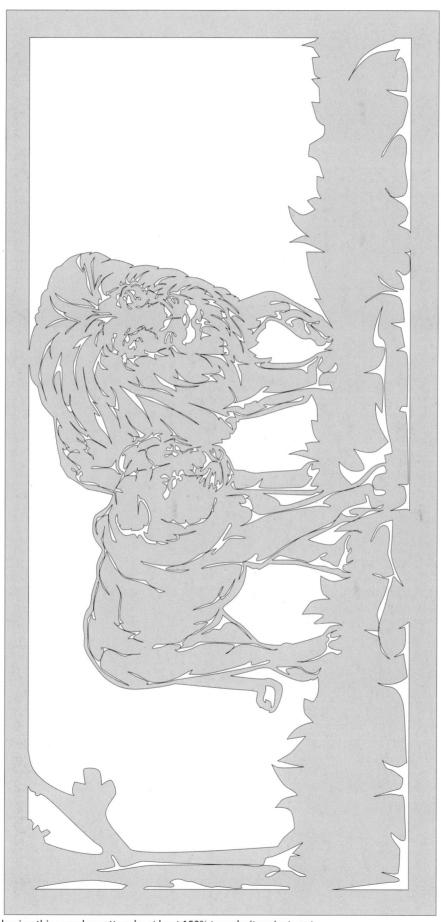

Note: We recommend enlarging this complex pattern by at least 150% to make it easier to cut.

Sun King — Lion

Hunting Lioness

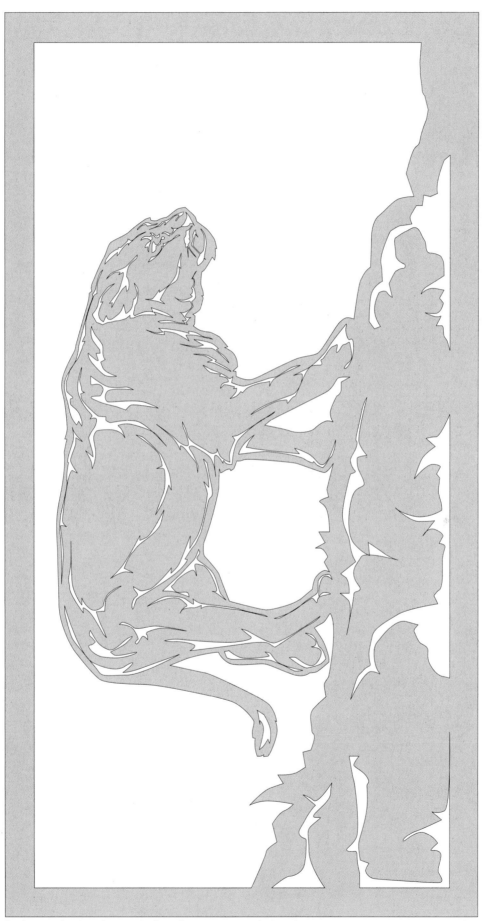

Note: We recommend enlarging this complex pattern by at least 150% to make it easier to cut.

Lioness in the Shade

Mountain Lion on the Prowl

Cheetah in the Shade

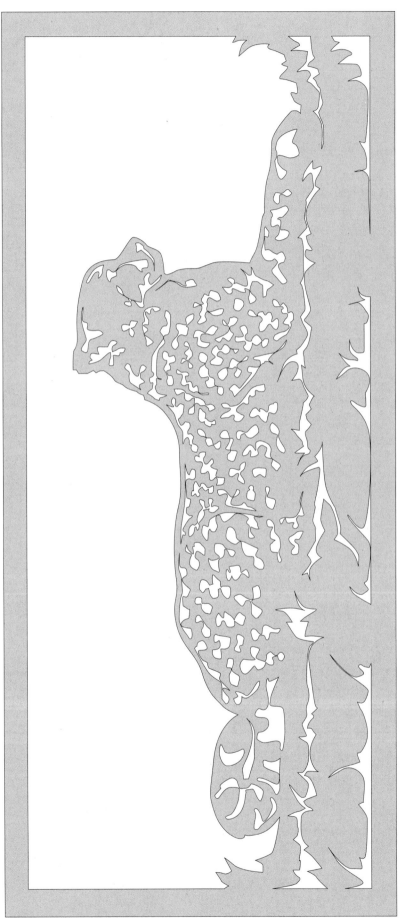

Note: We recommend enlarging this complex pattern by at least 150% to make it easier to cut.

Cheetah on Guard

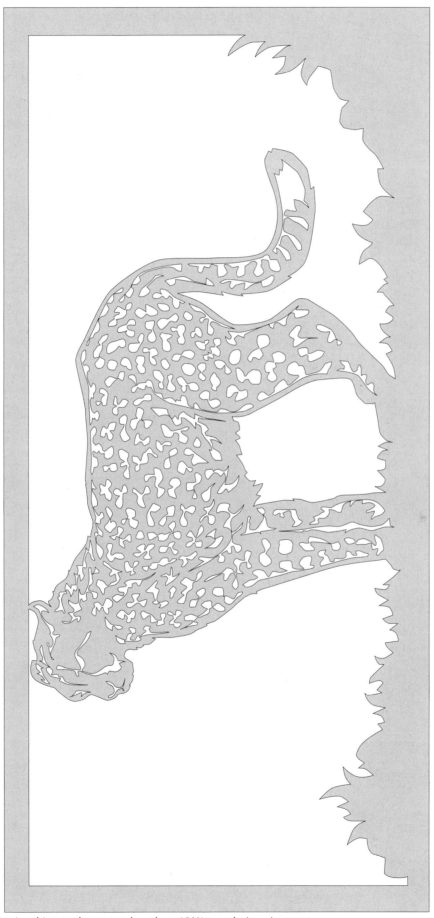

Note: We recommend enlarging this complex pattern by at least 150% to make it easier to cut.

Cheetah Portrait

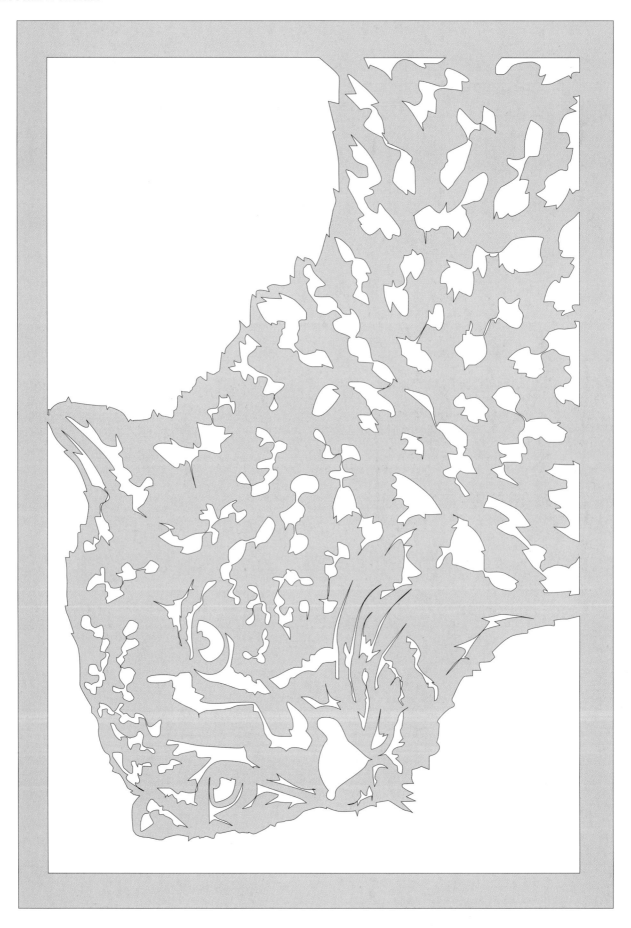

Mother Cougar

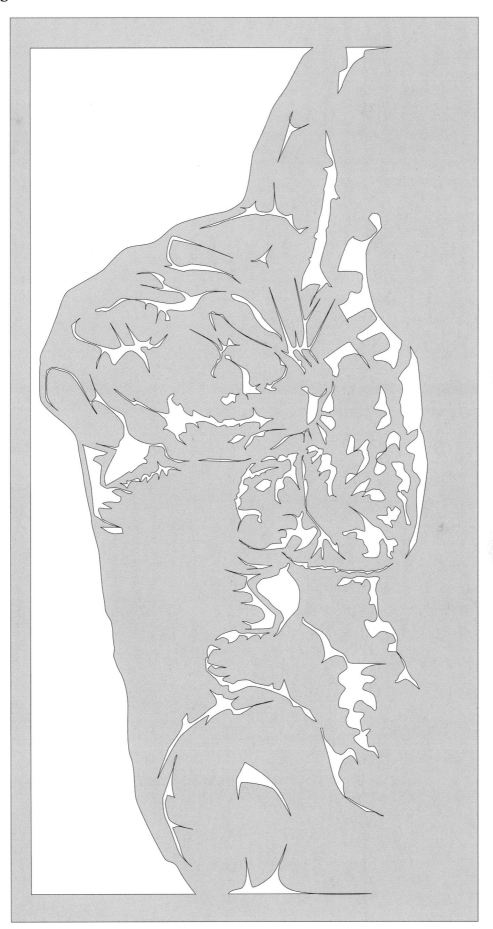

Pacing Cougar

Jaguar Resting

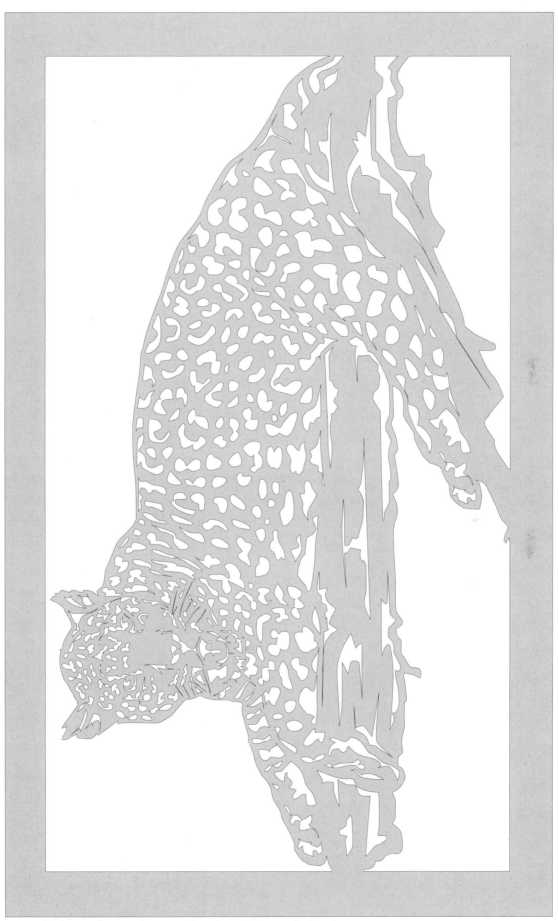

Note: We recommend enlarging this complex pattern by at least 150% to make it easier to cut.

Jaguar Portrait

Leopard on a Rock

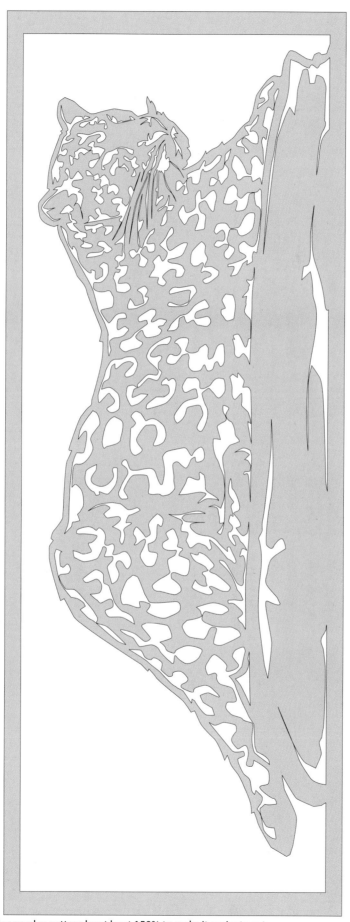

Note: We recommend enlarging this complex pattern by at least 150% to make it easier to cut.

Watchful Leopard

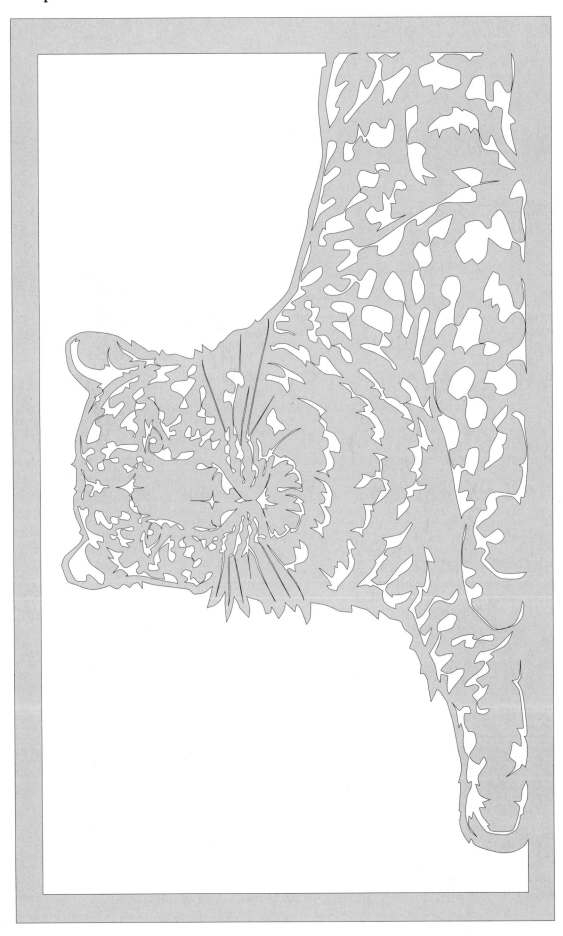

Distracted Leopard

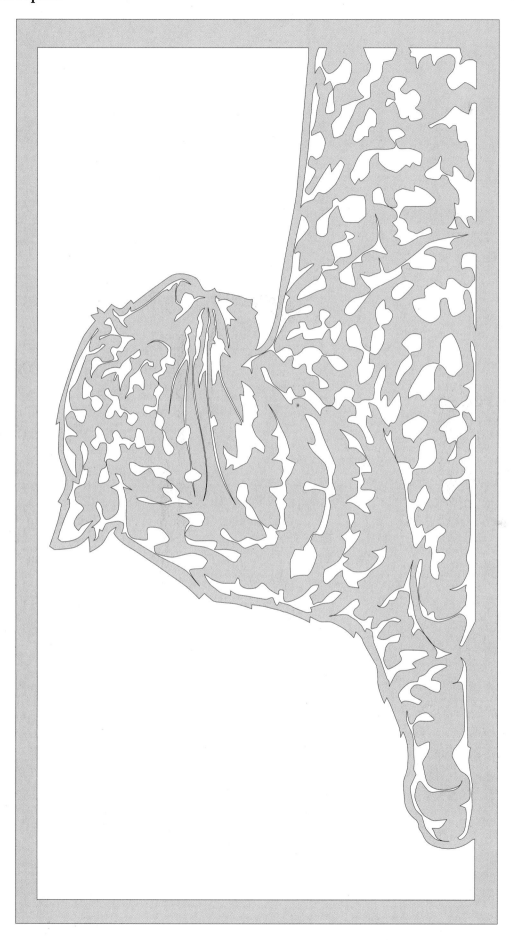

Predators

Wolf Stare

(See photo page 9.)

Wolf Pair

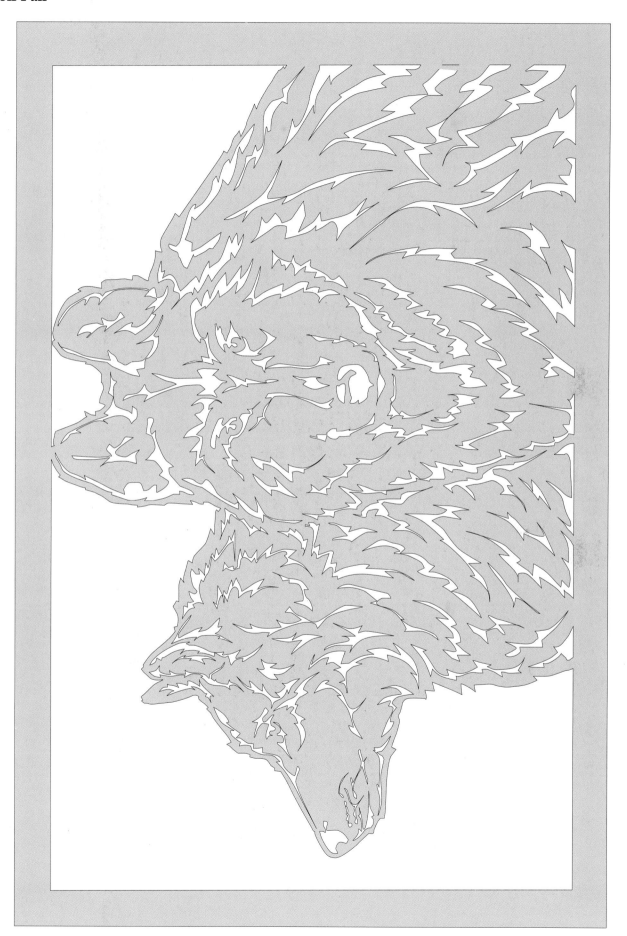

Wolf Snarl

Gray Wolf

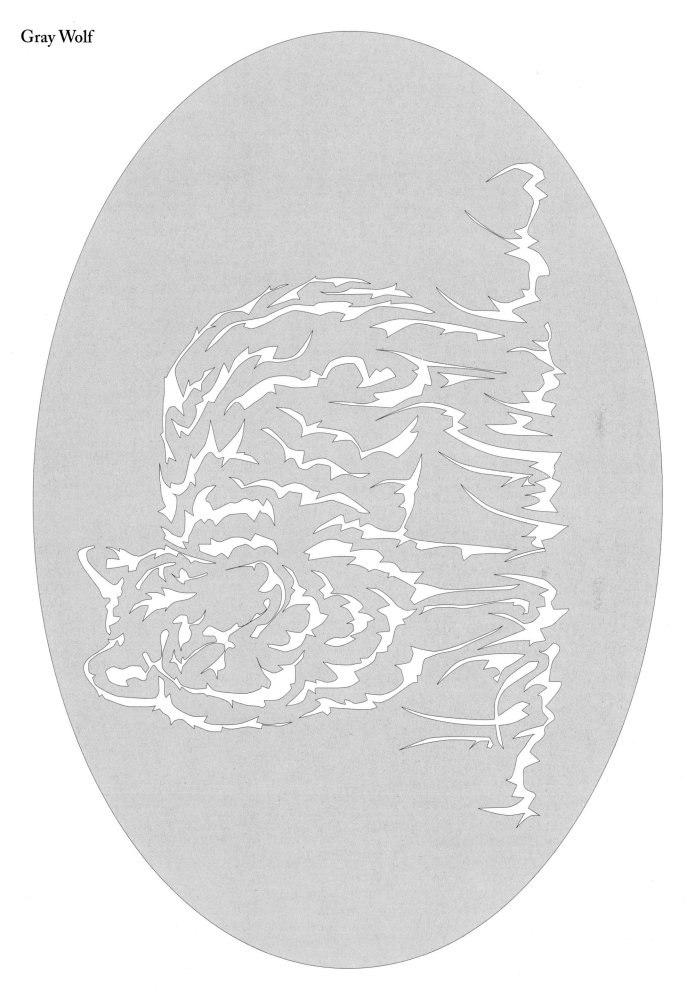

Wolf Attack

Summer Wolf

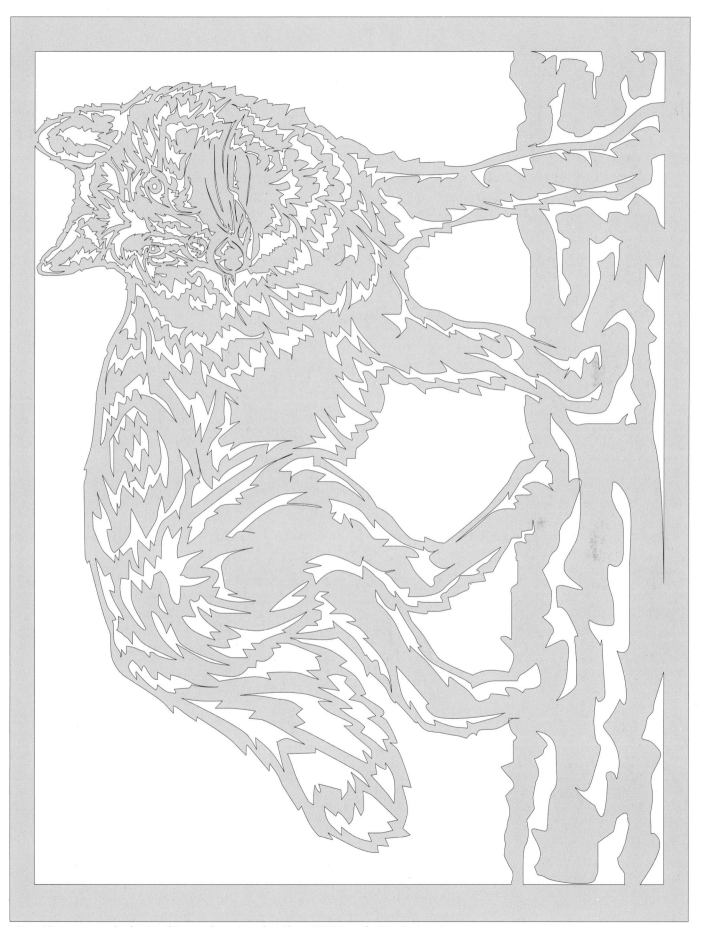

Note: We recommend enlarging this complex pattern by at least 150% to make it easier to cut.

Summer Wolf Portrait

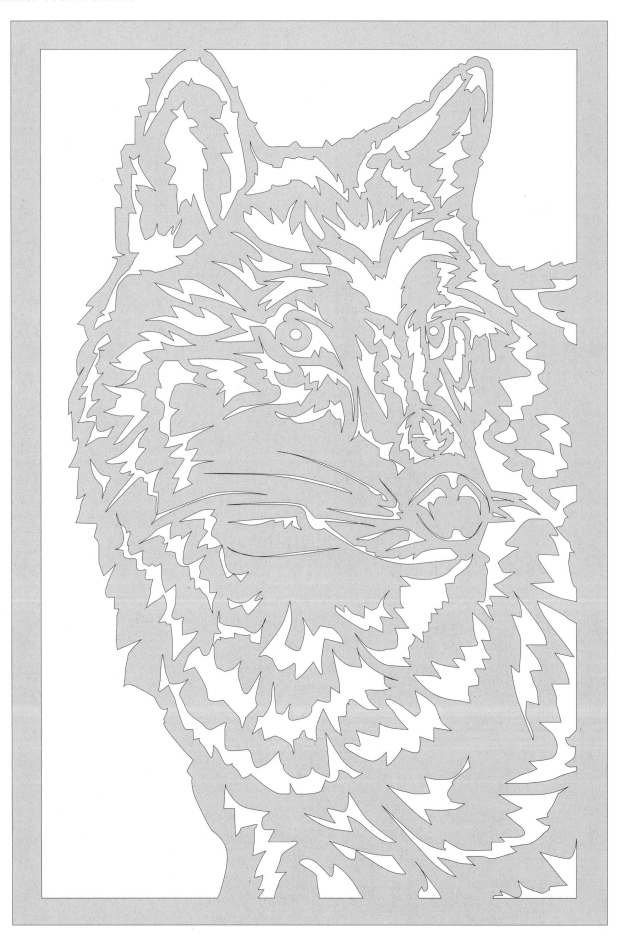

Dire Wolf

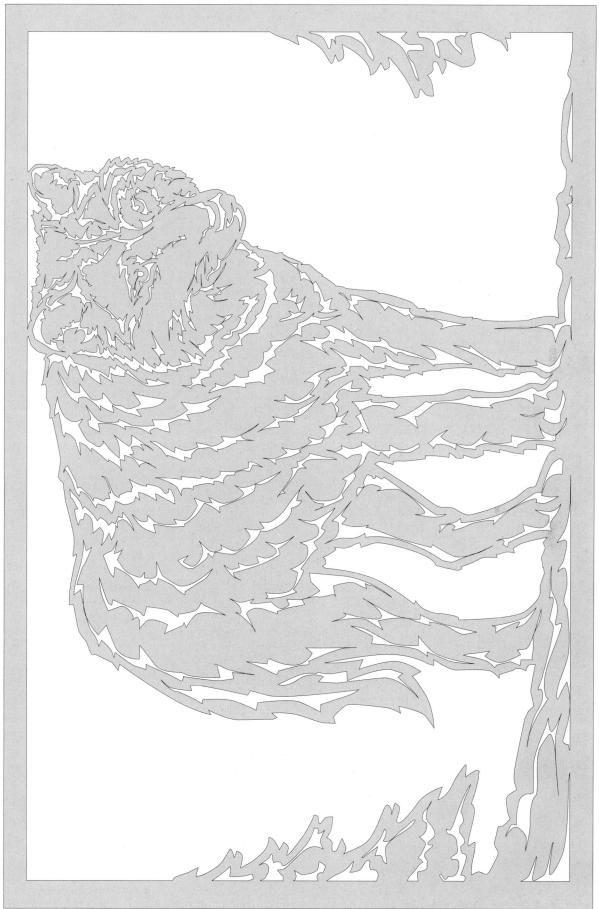

Note: We recommend enlarging this complex pattern by at least 150% to make it easier to cut. (See photo page 9.)

Wolf Portrait

Polar Bear Walking

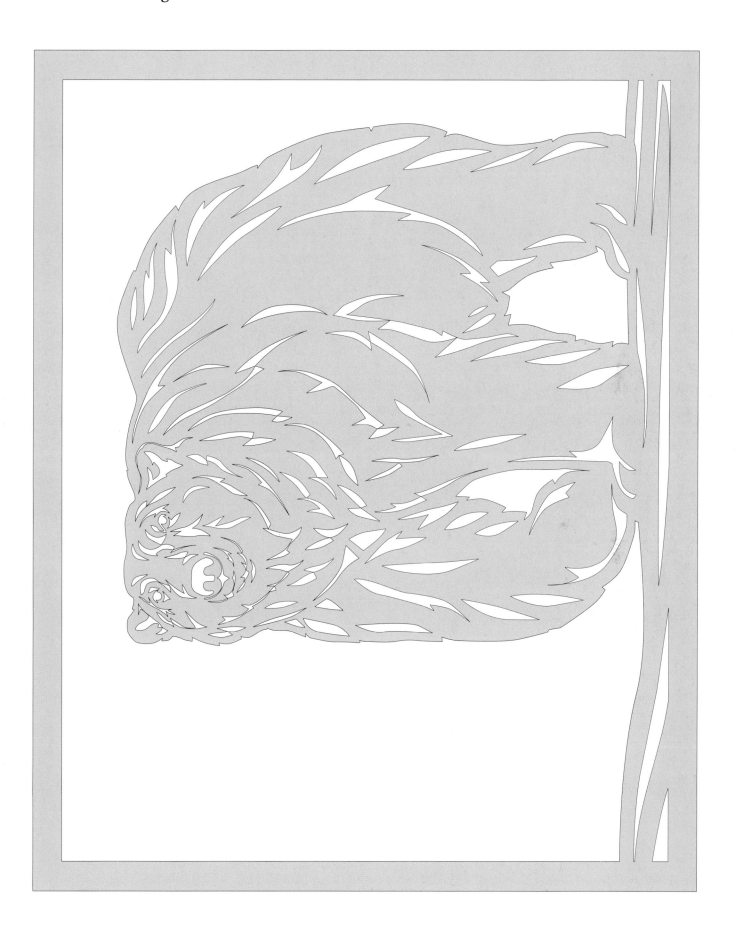

Polar Bear

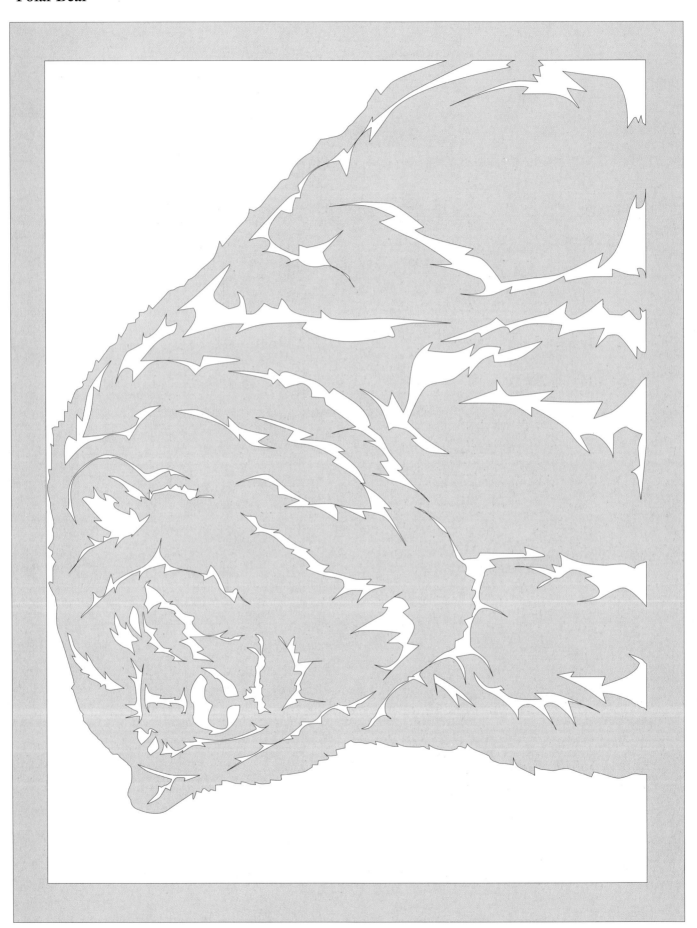

Bear Side Profile

Coyote Oval

Black Bear with Cubs

Note: We recommend enlarging this complex pattern by at least 150% to make it easier to cut.

Bear Roar

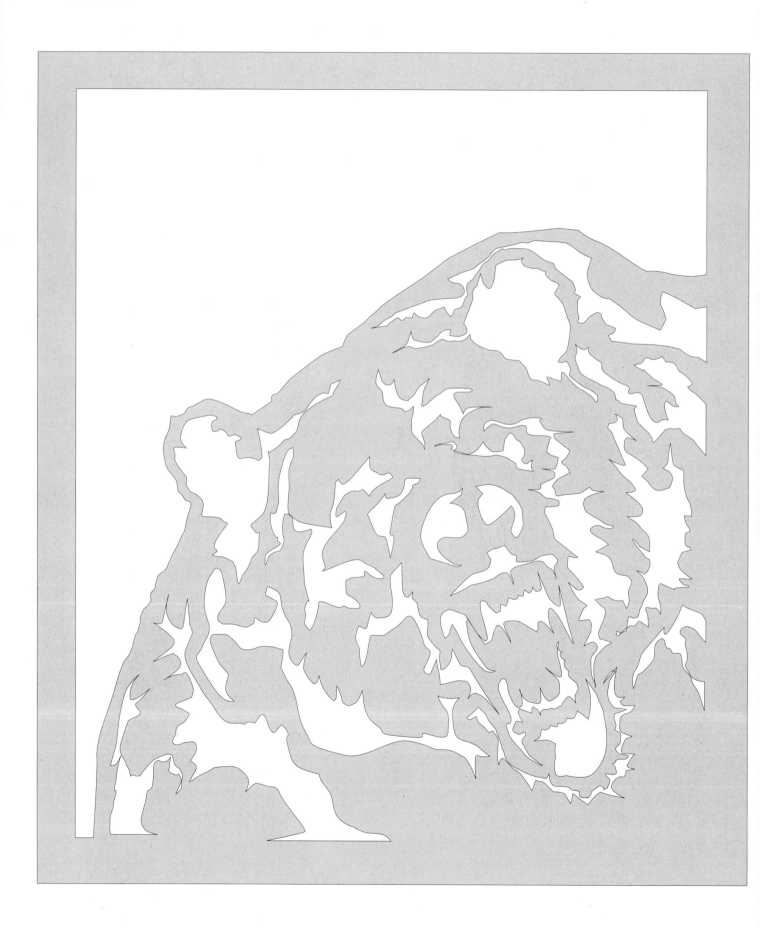

Bear on the Rocks

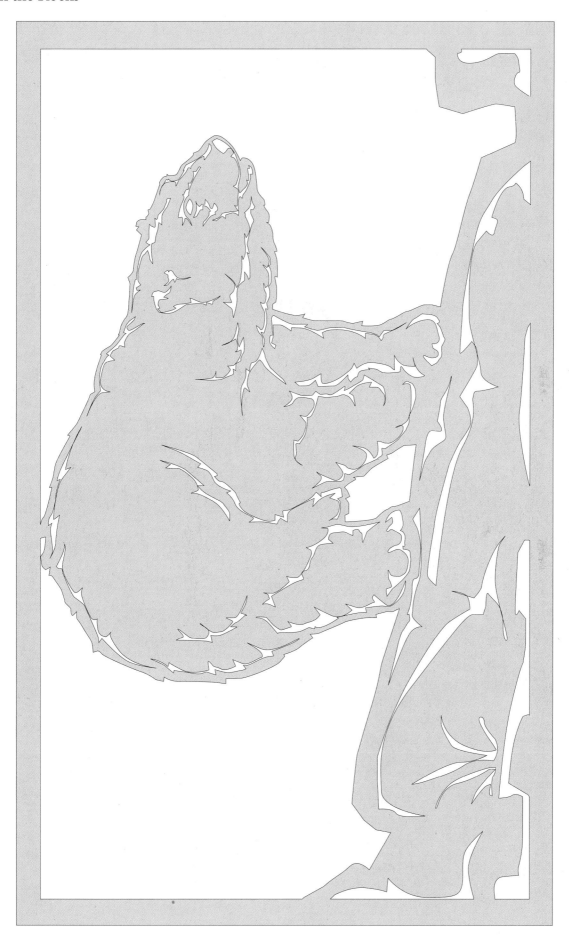

Wolf Oval Profile

Red Fox

Florida Alligator

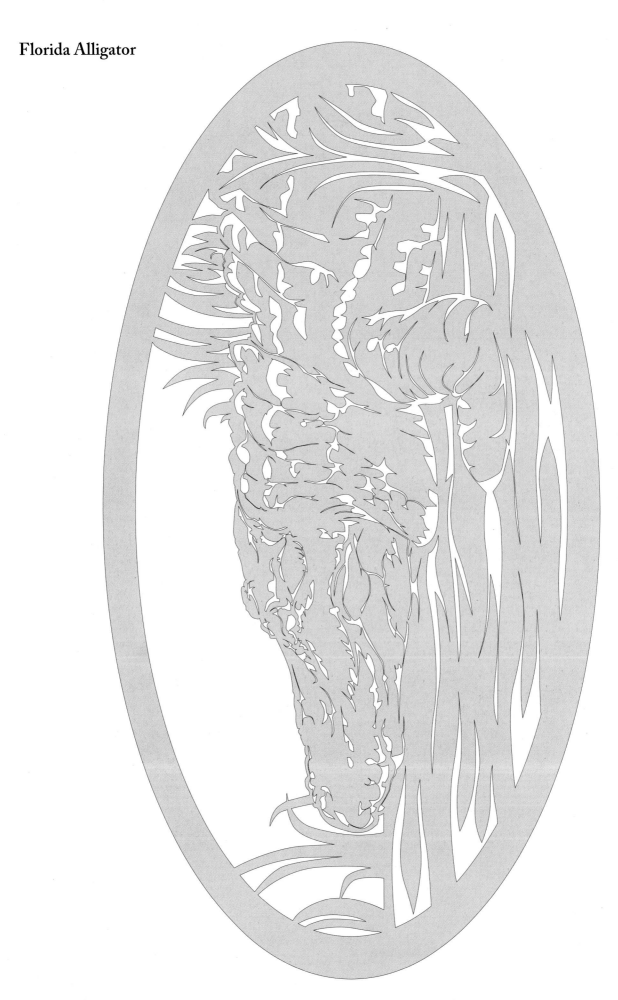

Birds of Prey

Bald Eagle Portrait

(See photo page 13.)

Bald Eagle Perching

Note: We recommend enlarging this complex pattern by at least 150% to make it easier to cut.

Bald Eagle in Flight

Golden Eagle

(See photo page 12.)

Young Great Horned Owl

Barn Owl with Mouse

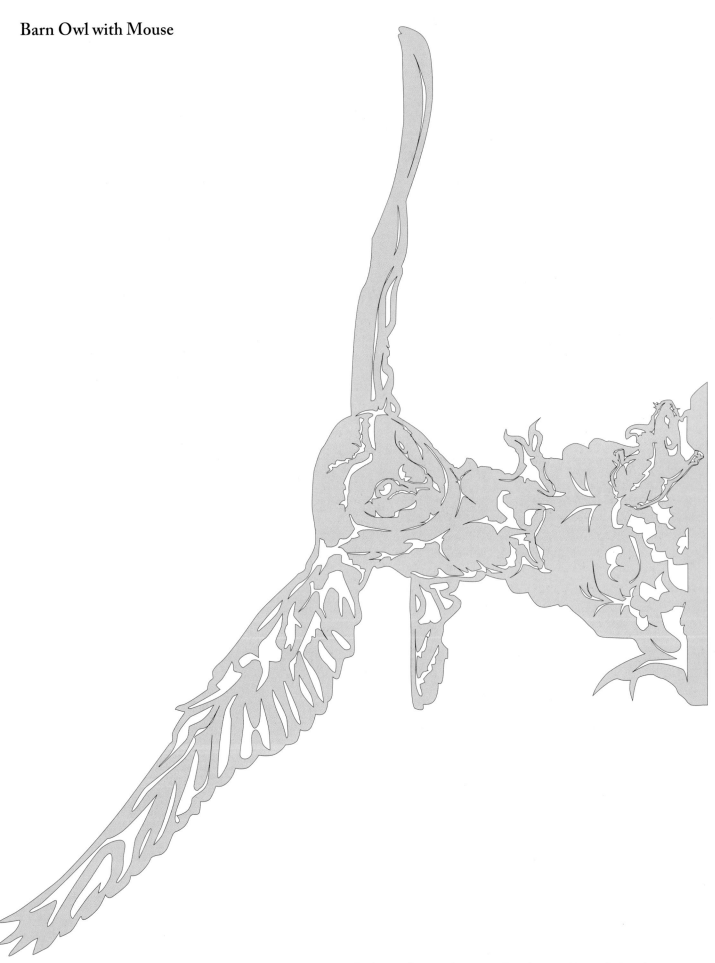

Note: We recommend enlarging this complex pattern by at least 150% to make it easier to cut.

Sitting Barn Owl

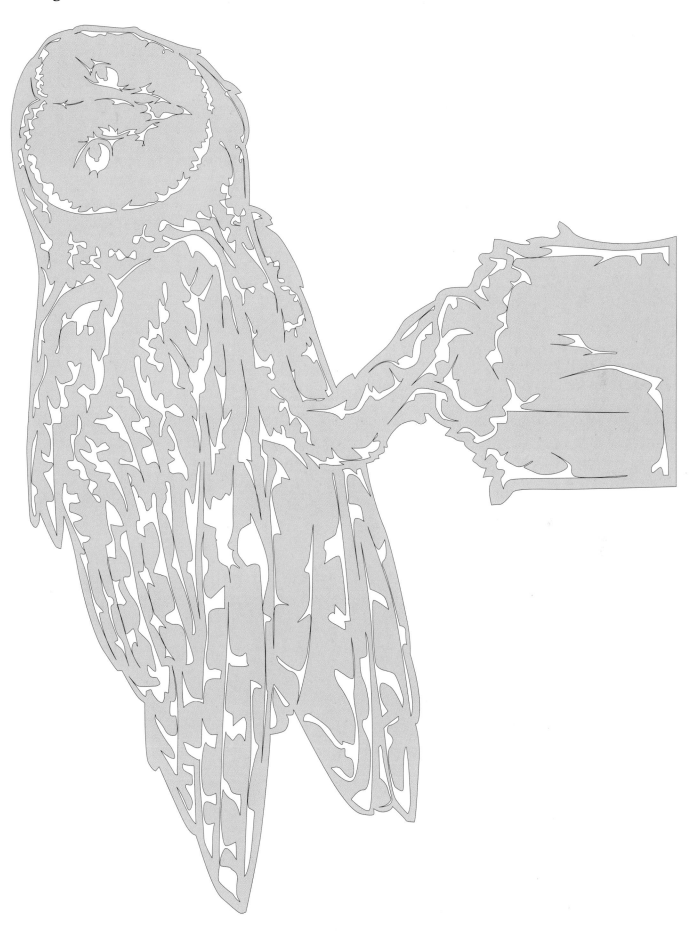

Eagle Owl

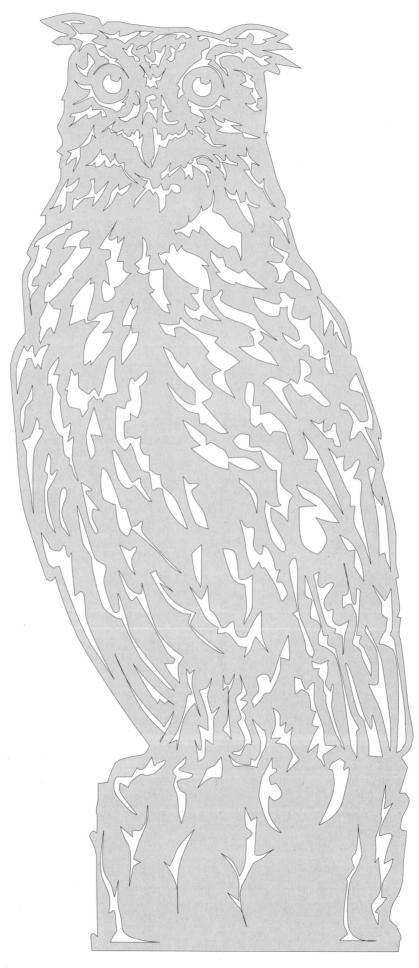

Screech Owl

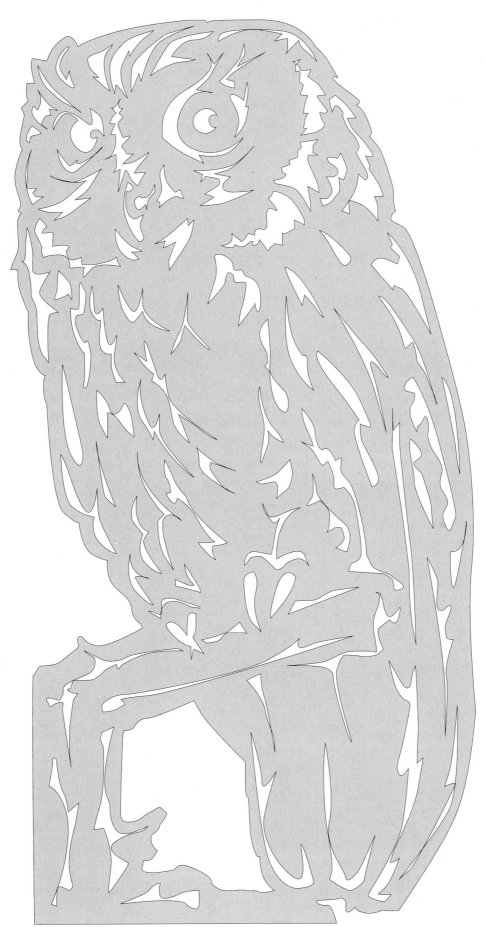

(See photo page 13.)

Small Owl

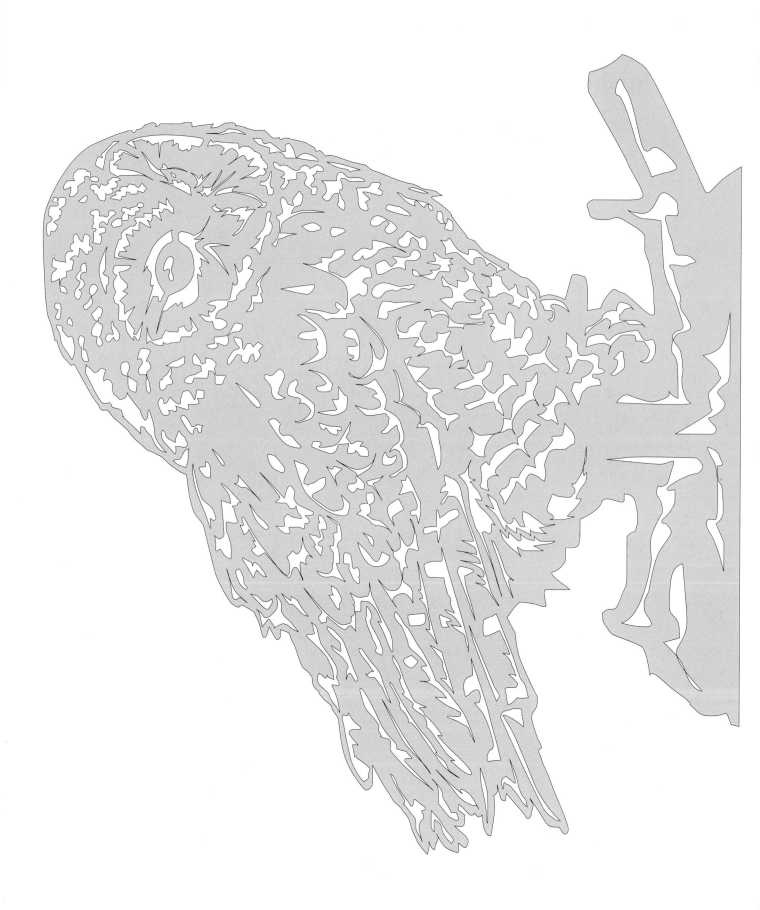

Ferruginous Hawk

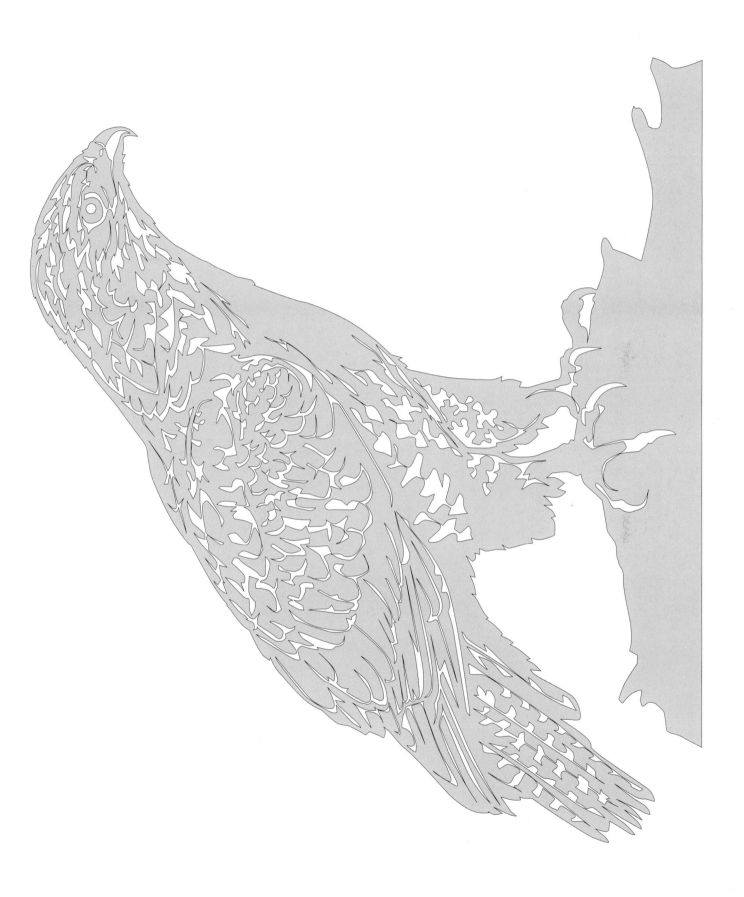

Harris Hawk

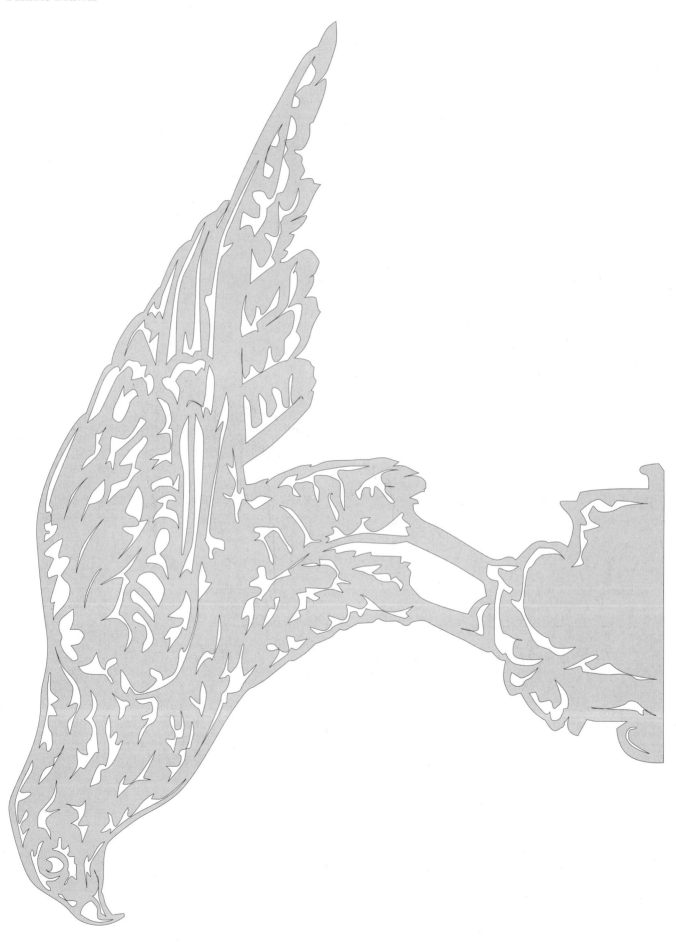

Red-Tailed Hawk

Falcon

Peregrine Falcon

Osprey with Dinner

Sanibel Osprey Taking Off

Note: We recommend enlarging this complex pattern by at least 150% to make it easier to cut.

Sparrow Hawk

Backyard Animals

American Robin

Raccoon

Grey Squirrel

Loon (Simple)

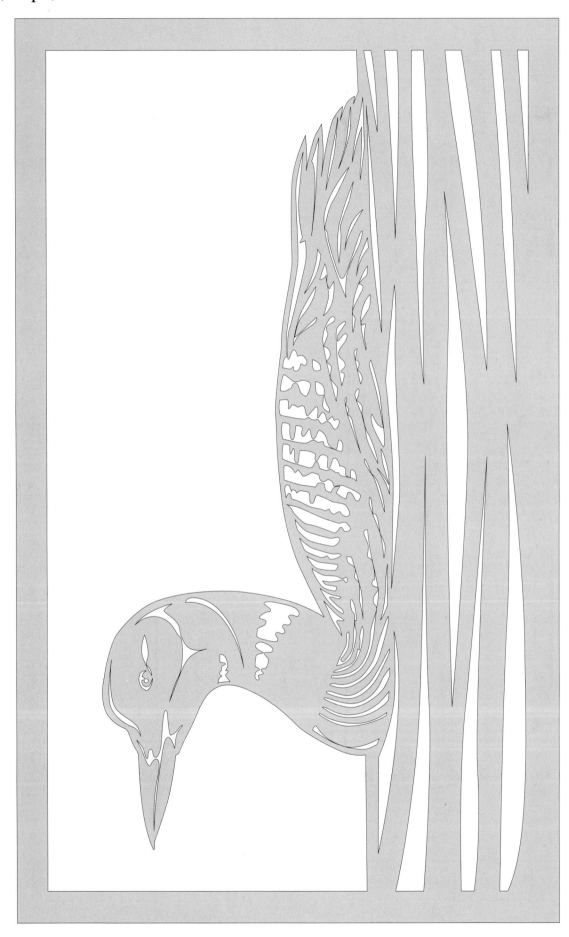

Loon (Complex)

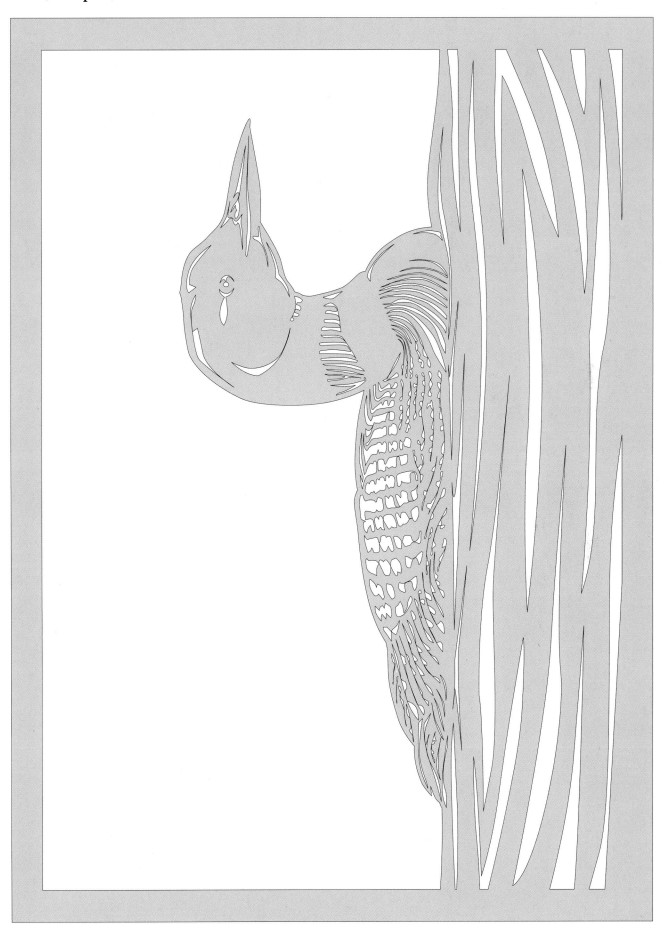

Royal Tern

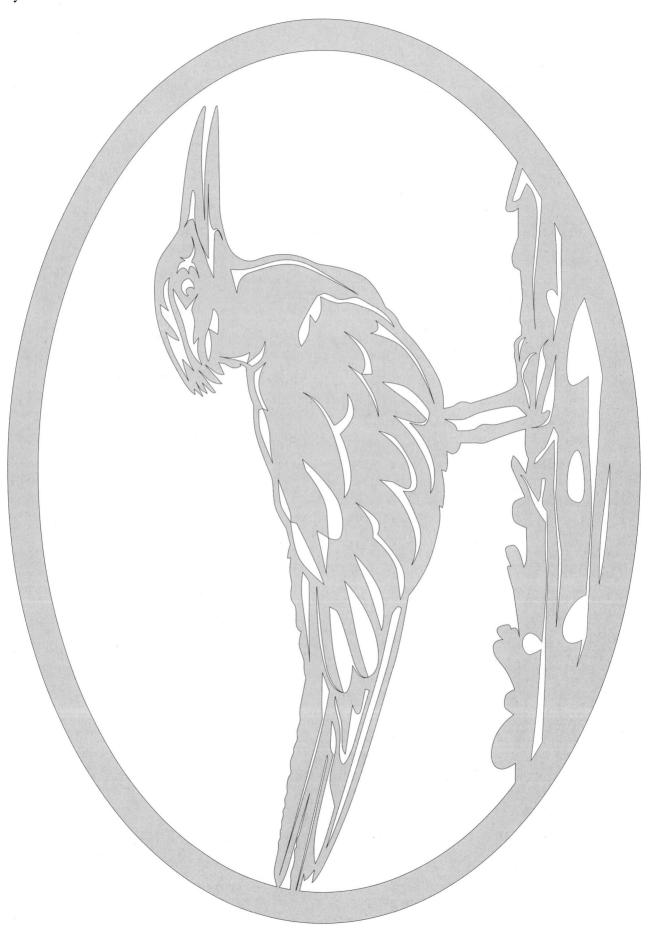

Sandwich Tern

Ruby-Throated Hummingbird

Snowy Plover

Bighorn Sheep

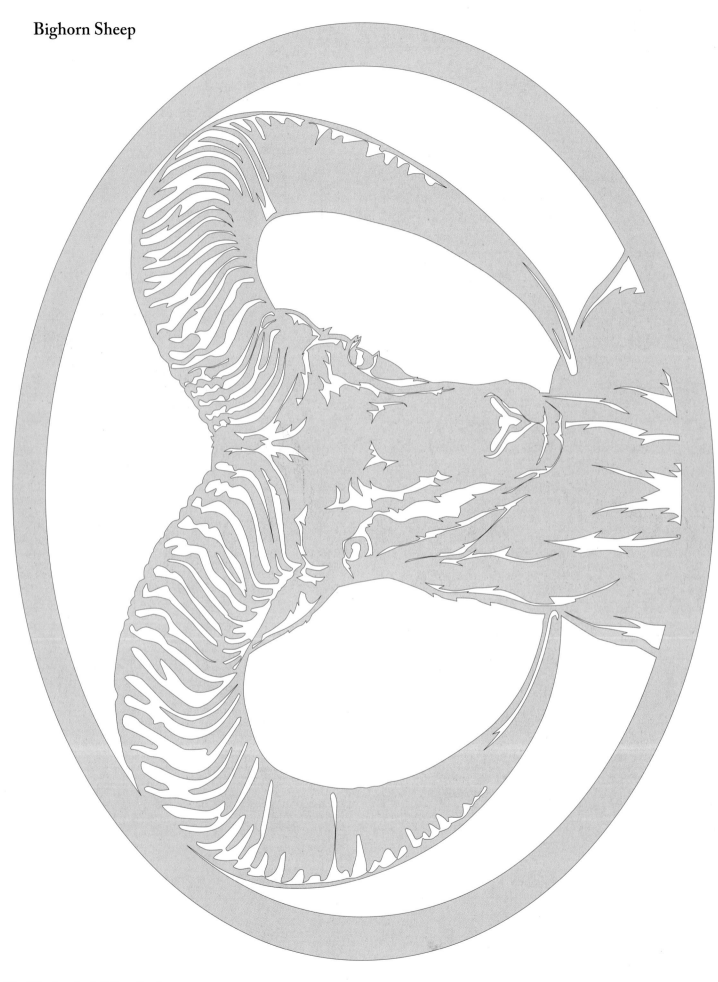

Bison Roaming

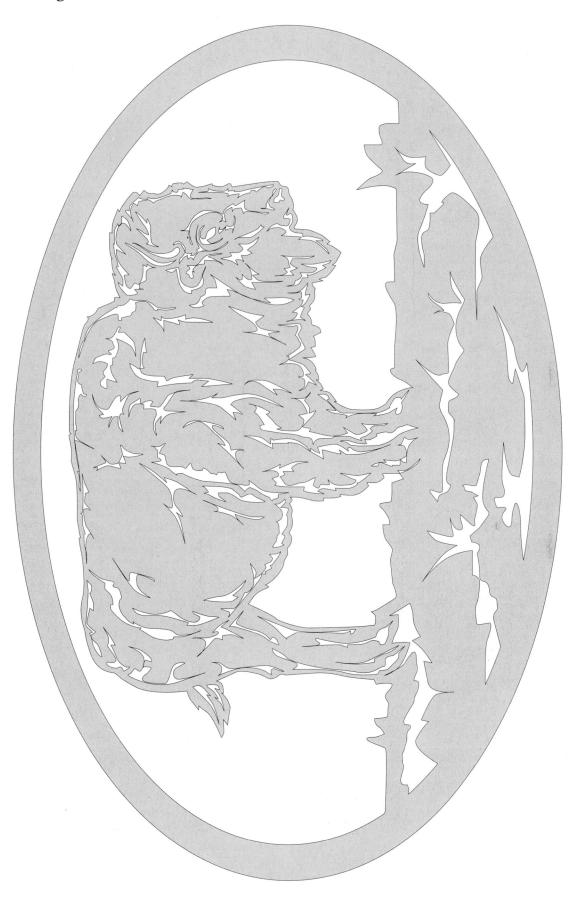

Delicate Fawn

(See photo page 17.)

Majestic Buck

(See photo page 14.)

Black-Tailed Deer

Forest-Dwelling Moose

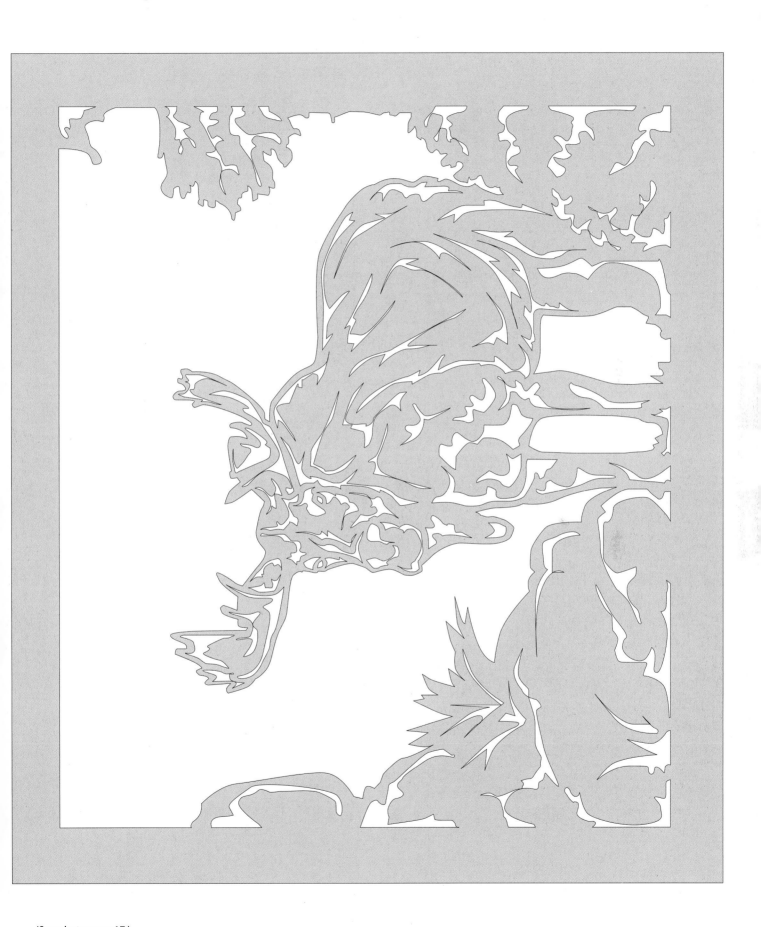

(See photo page 17.)

Running Horse

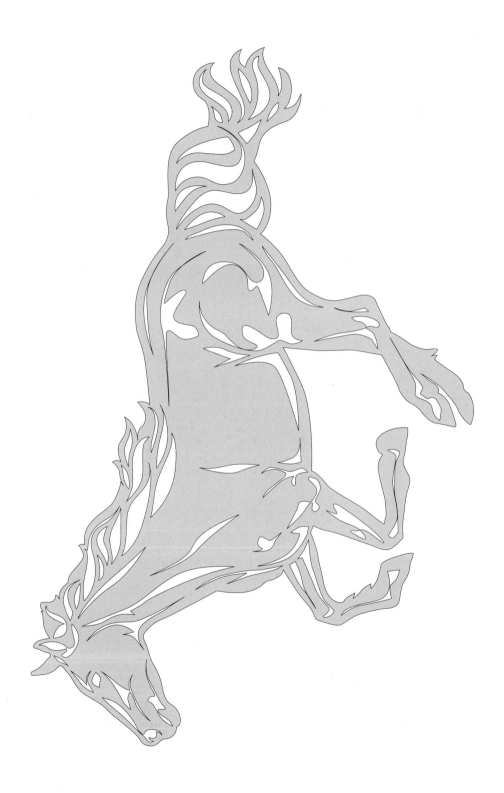

Wild Horse Galloping Free

Bass-Voice Bullfrog

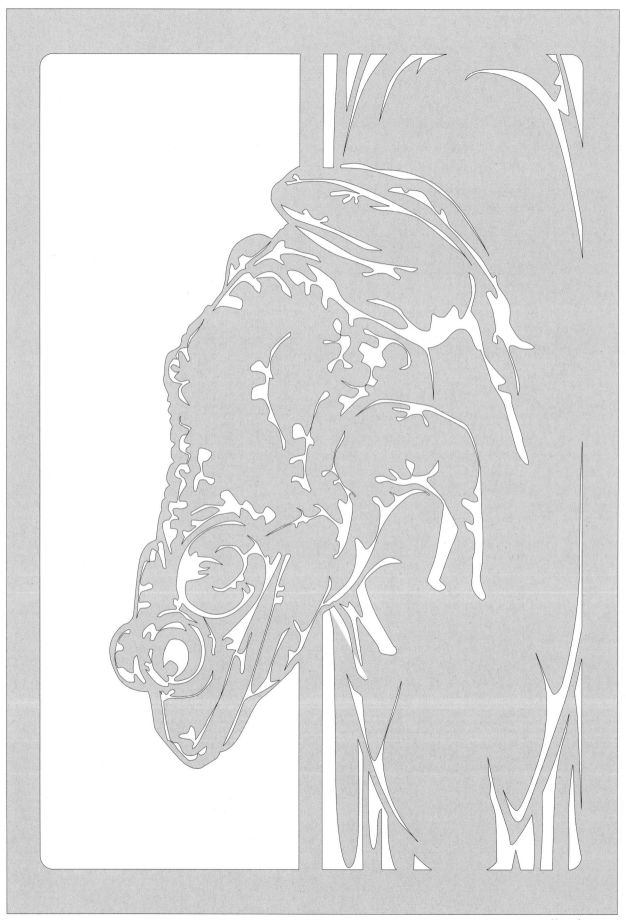

(See photo page 10.)

Cottage Chipmunk

Eastern Massauga Rattlesnake

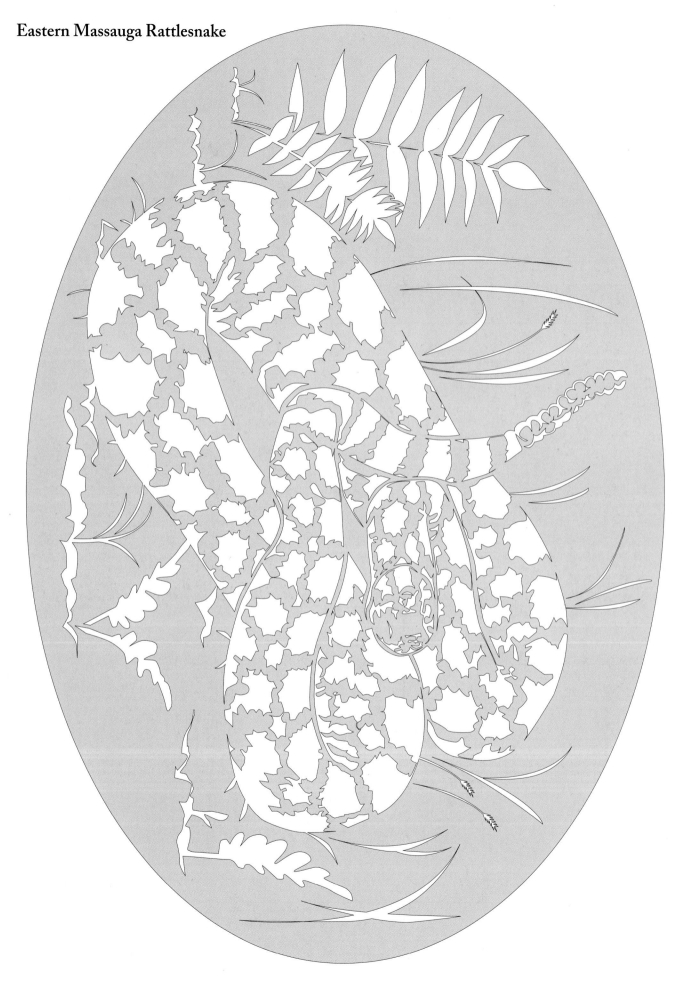

Jackrabbit with Base

(See photo page 16.)

Exotic Animals

Cape Buffalo Portrait

Wallowing Hippo

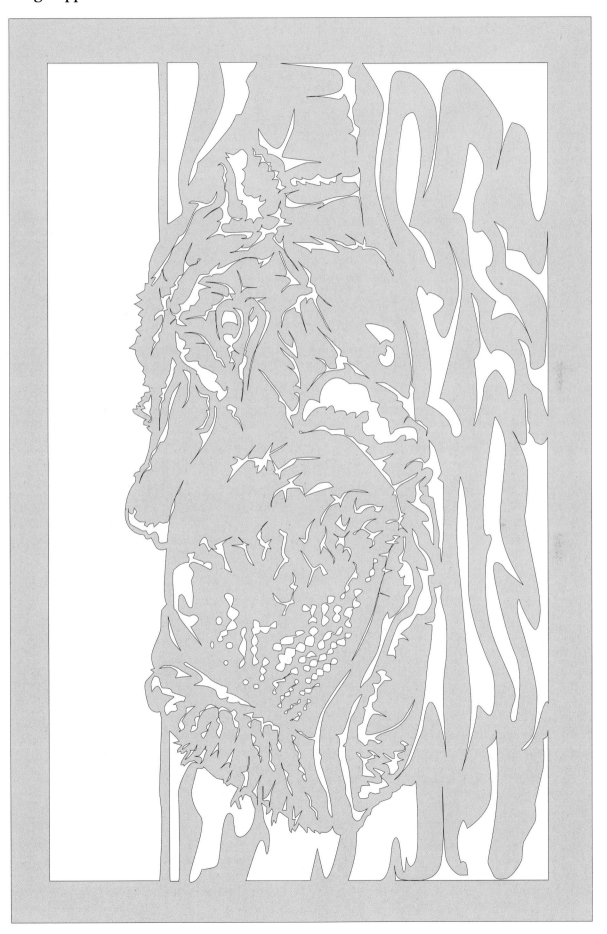

Wood Stork

Giraffe Mother and Child

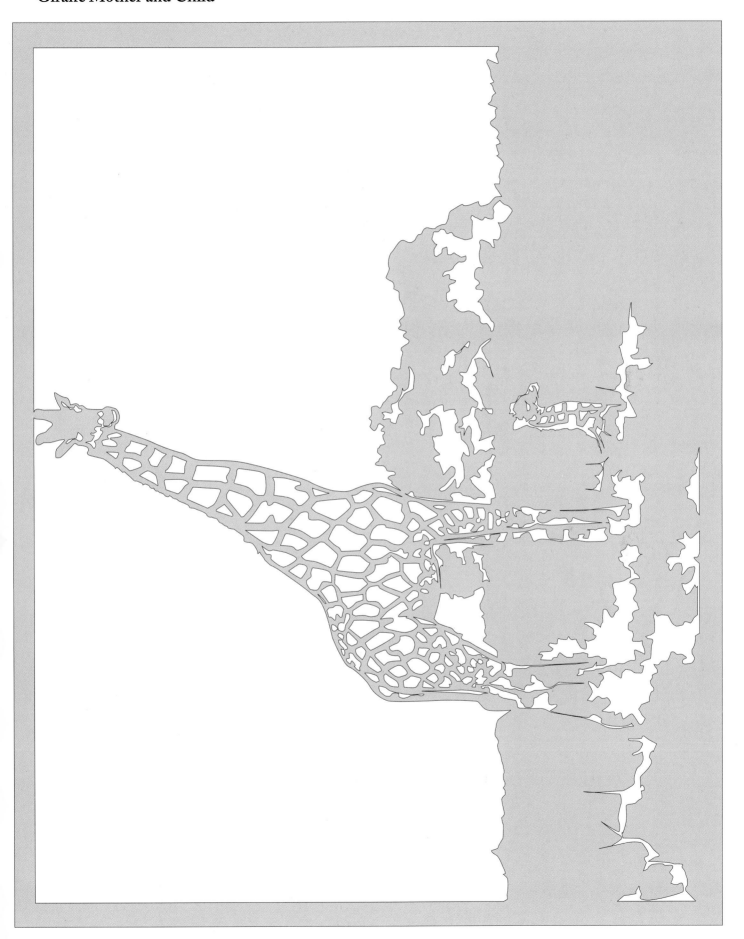

Giraffe Bust

(See photo page 20.)

Toucan

Shy Gorilla

(See photo page 19.)

Ostrich — Feathered but Flightless

African Penguin

Gentoo Penguin

Wary Rhinoceros

(See photo page 116.)

Kangaroo

Savanna Stripes — Zebra

(See photo page 10.)

Florida Tricolored Heron

Desert Camels

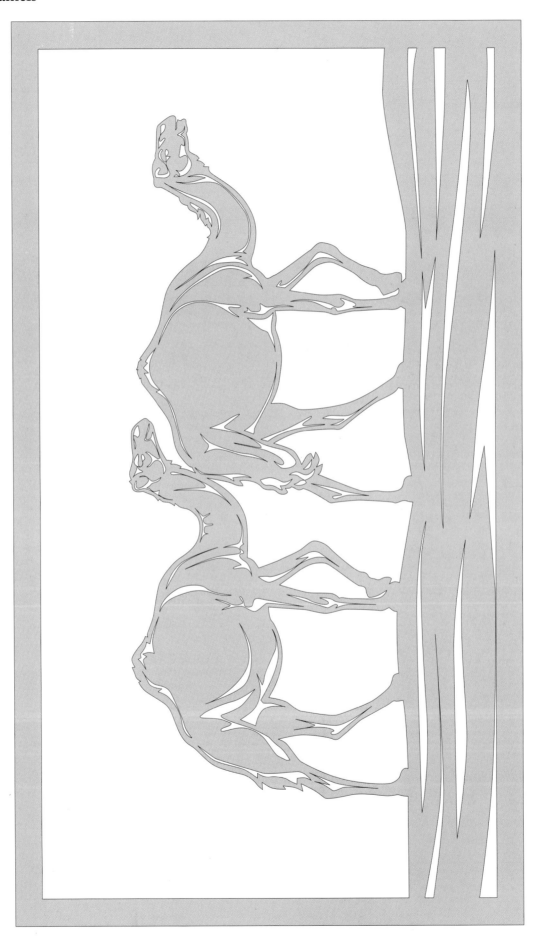

River Hippo Walking

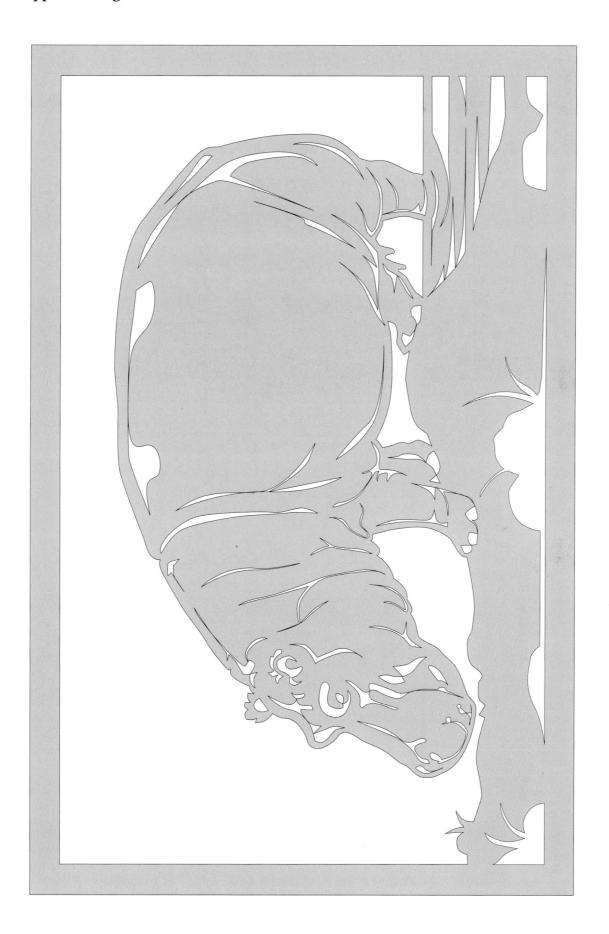

Gentle Giant — African Elephant

Indian Elephant Mother and Child

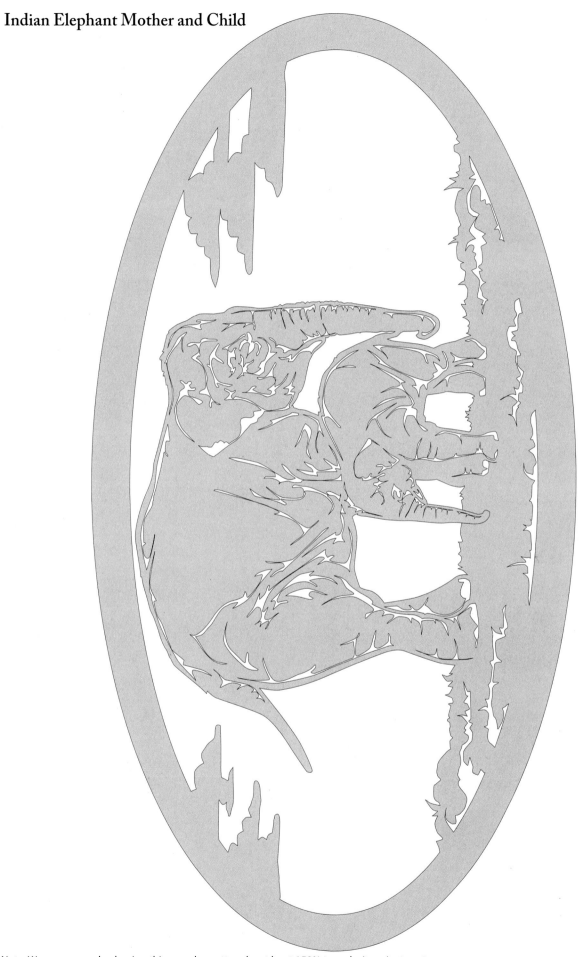

Note: We recommend enlarging this complex pattern by at least 150% to make it easier to cut.

Bamboo Bear — Giant Panda

White Rhino

Koala Bear

Peacock Resplendent

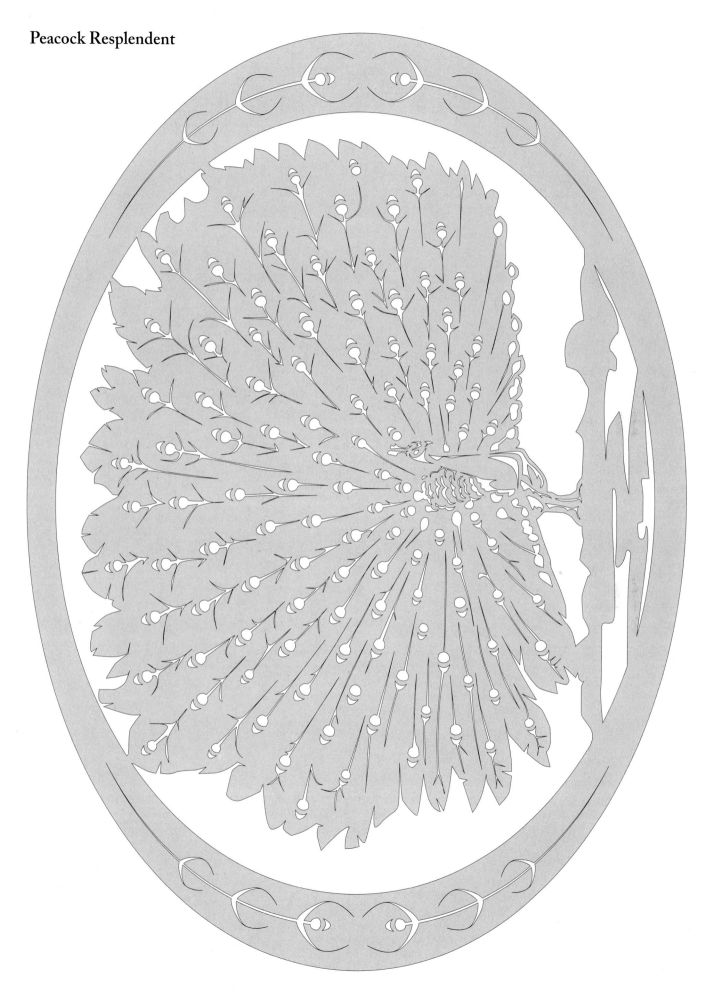

Index

Page numbers in *italics* indicate patterns. Page numbers in **bold** indicate Gallery items.